BRANCH LINES AROUND WISBECH

from Peterborough, Sutton Bridge, March, Watlington and Upwell

Andrew C Ingram

Series editor Vic Mitchell

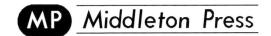

MP Middleton Press

This album is dedicated to Wisbech engine drivers Albert South and Charlie Rand.

Published November 1997

ISBN 1 901706 01 X

© Middleton Press

Design Deborah Goodridge

Published by
  Middleton Press
  Easebourne Lane
  Midhurst, West Sussex
  GU29 9AZ
Tel: 01730 813169   Fax: 01730 812601

Printed & bound by Biddles Ltd,
  Guildford and Kings Lynn

CONTENTS

INDEX

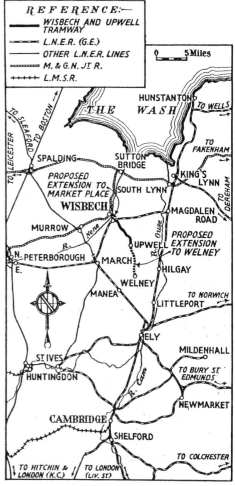

(1937 Railway Magazine)

ACKNOWLEDGEMENTS

In addition to information supplied by the photographers I am most grateful to the following for their assistance in the preparation of this book: G.Arundel, C.Atkin, C.Awdry, J.Barker, R.Bell, A.Boston, K.Bowden, J.Carter, D.Cullen, M.Elston, P.Foster, J.Fox, Rev D.Fysh, C.Garford, A.G.W.Garraway, D.Geldard, P.Hunt, J.Ingram, G.Kenworthy, C.Payne, T.Pleasance, N.Rand, R.Randall, D.Rayner, E.Shinkin, P.Waszak, P.Wright, the staff at Cambridgeshire Collection, National Railway Museum, Peterborough Central Library, Wisbech District Library, Wisbech Harbour Office and Wisbech & Fenland Museum.

GEOGRAPHICAL SETTING

The absence of contour lines around Wisbech is not indicative of a boring, featureless landscape.

A medieval abbey at Thorney, the 12th century cathedral at Peterborough, and fine Norman churches in Walsoken and Wisbech, bear testament to early settlement in this once inhospitable fenland. An extensive system of natural and man-made waterways, to keep the reclaimed Fenland marshes dry, provided the only efficient means of transporting goods before the advent of railways.

The rich fertile soils support one of the most important agricultural and horticultural areas in Britain, with produce picked, cooked, canned and stored in Wisbech. Regular produce auctions and twice-weekly market are held in Wisbech, with additional markets in March and Peterborough.

Tourism has become an important service industry in Fenland, which encompasses parts of Lincolnshire, Cambridgeshire and West Norfolk. The well-stocked waterways, where once fenmen made their living, now regularly host national angling championships. Historic houses, churches and windmills stand proud against the distant horizon, where panoramic skies offer breathtaking sunsets.

This album marks the 150th anniversary of Wisbech railways. Not just straight rails across a flat landscape, but a once extensive and fascinating system around this Historic Capital of The Fens.

All the maps are from the 1901-03 edition, to the scale of 25ins to 1 mile, unless otherwise shown. North is at the top of the maps, except where indicated with an arrow.

1946 map at nearly 4 miles to 1 inch.

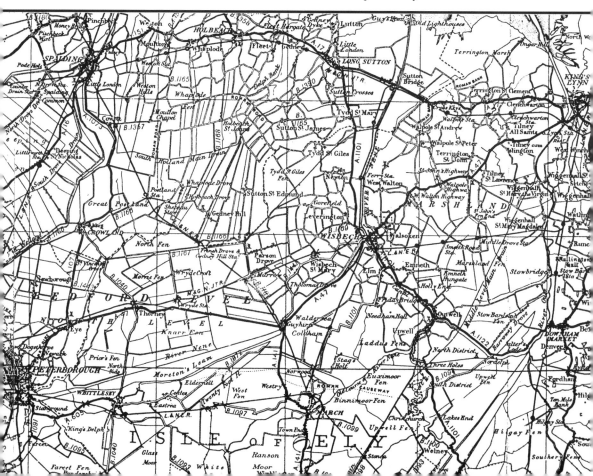

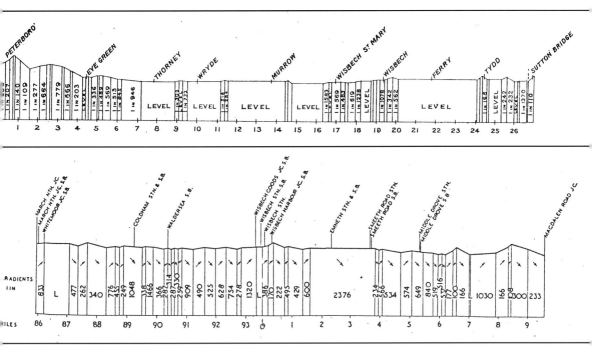

HISTORICAL BACKGROUND

The railway age began at Wisbech on 3rd May 1847, when the Wisbech, St Ives and Cambridge Junction Railway Company, assisted by the Eastern Counties Railway, opened the branch from March to Wisbech. In that same year the Lynn & Ely Railway commenced work on a branch line from their line at Watlington, to join the ECR line at Wisbech.

On 6th November 1847 the *Wisbech Advertiser* observed that "As there appears to be a misunderstanding between the East Anglian and Eastern Counties Companies, the former will not run to the station of the latter, but will proceed immediately to the erection of a temporary station in Mr Shepherd's field in Gaol Lane". The line opened on 1st February 1848, but this disagreement over operating rights continued. In August 1851 the paper reported that "On the morning of the 10th [July], on the arrival of the first train from Lynn to Peterborough at the East Anglian station at Wisbech, it was found impracticable for the train to proceed any further in consequence of the Eastern Counties having blocked the line by placing a train of wagons across the junction of the Eastern Counties and East Anglian lines, the points for turning the trains upon the

latter line having been taken up in the course of the night." This dispute was finally resolved when the EAR was absorbed by the ECR on 1st January 1852, which in turn became part of the newly-formed Great Eastern Railway on 7th August 1862.

Powers for a Harbour branch were obtained by the ECR in 1852, but ten years elapsed before the Wisbech Advertiser reported the first train on 11th November 1862. "The line was worked on Tuesday morning, a train of trucks passing over it with a quantity of timber trees which had been found by the side of the line, and a stack of hay which was grown on the land over which it passes. We hear there is a probability of an agreement being made with some Derbyshire coalowners to ship coals here for exportation".

The Peterborough, Wisbeach and Sutton Bridge Railway opened for goods on 1st June 1866, with passenger services commencing two months later. Starting at Peterborough GNR station, the line initially terminated at the low-level station in Sutton Bridge, opened by the Norwich and Spalding Railway on 1st July 1862. The Lynn & Sutton Bridge Railway opened their high-level station on 1st March 1866, with the low level station closing to passengers in January 1867.

The GNR invested a total of £55,000 in a major docks scheme at Sutton Bridge, to be served by a short branch from the Spalding line, west of Sutton Bridge Junction. The first vessel, Wisbech-registered Garland, docked on Saturday 14th May 1881 with 1,500 tons of Norwegian pine for English Brothers. Problems arose within twenty-four hours, as serious subsidence by the lock gates threatened the ship. She managed to sail with a cargo of Derbyshire coal, the first and last departure, as Sutton Bridge dock was subsequently abandoned. The Peterborough to Sutton Bridge branch was absorbed by the Eastern & Midlands Railway from 1st July 1883, and the new Midland & Great Northern Joint Railway on 1st July 1893.

The Great Eastern Railway opened their standard gauge railway from Wisbech to Outwell on 20th August 1883. The Upwell terminus of this six-mile branch received its first traffic on 8th September 1884. Built and operated by the GER, within the provisions of the 1870 Tramways Act, the Wisbech & Upwell Tramway had a unique appeal. Passengers sat in tramcars on longitudinal bench seats, hauled by wooden-bodied locomotives, travelling at an average 6mph.

Goods trains, also worked by tram locomotives, carried fruit, flowers and sugar beet in conventional rolling stock.

In 1923 the GER became a constituent of the London & North Eastern Railway, who with the LMS jointly operated the M&GN route. Tramway passenger services were withdrawn from 2nd January 1928 by the LNER, who took sole control of the M&GN on 1st October 1936.

All the lines were nationalised on 1st January 1948. When British Railways began painting long-neglected crossing gates and signalboxes around Wisbech, closure notices soon followed. Passenger services through Wisbech North ceased from 2nd March 1959, with the goods yard and harbour branch closing from 28th December 1964. The GER harbour branch closed on 12th September 1966, followed two years later by the Watlington to Wisbech line from 9th September 1968. The first railway into Wisbech had become the last.

In 1995 Wisbech Town Council submitted a FenRail Project to the Millennium Commission. This scheme, which envisaged reopening the branch to passenger traffic and reinstating the Down line at Coldham as a passing loop, was eventually rejected by the Commission.

PASSENGER SERVICES

GER Routes

On 3rd May 1847 an excursion train to Cambridge, with a 1st class return fare of 6/-, marked the formal opening of the railway in Wisbech. Initially the passenger service to March consisted of five weekday and two Sunday trains. The East Anglian Railways timetable for February 1848 showed departures to King's Lynn at 10am, 12 noon, and 5.30pm, with 10am and 7pm trains running on a Sunday.

The Eastern Counties Railway were not renowned for their timekeeping. Wisbechians paid them a doubtful compliment by saying that trains were as slow as the Wisbech church clock, which was then under repair.

The table below indicates the train frequency but omits services operating only on one day a week.

	From March		From Watlington	
	Weekdays	Sundays	Weekdays	Sundays
1870	8	1	3	-
1890	15	2	3	-
1910	17	2	5	-
1930	13	3	9	-
1950	12	5	7	-

The GER timetable for August 1915 recorded ten weekday departures to King's Lynn between 7.52am and 1.26am, with eleven return workings arriving between 7.44am and 11.02pm. Twelve trains ran to March, the first at 6.30am, with thirteen Down trains arriving back at Wisbech between 7.50am and 1.21am the following morning.

"The Fenman", introduced by British Railways in 1949, was the only named train service to work through Wisbech. The main portion ran from Hunstanton, whilst a feeder service, complete with headboard, ran from Wisbech to join the main train at Ely. In 1955, a special Sunday return fare of 12/- to London offered a 12.37pm arrival at Liverpool Street station, with an 8.24pm departure from the capital.

Through trains to Hunstanton, Cambridge and Peterborough still featured in the summer 1963 timetable, normally worked by a Brush Type 2 hauling corridor stock.

A variety of specials have since worked on the remaining March to Wisbech line. The most prestigious visit occurred in 1975, when the Royal Train was stabled overnight between Whitemoor Junction and Elm Road Crossing, March prior to HM The Queen attending a Maundy Thursday service at Peterborough Cathedral.

M&GN Routes

At 8.48am on 1st August 1866 the first passenger train left Wisbech station for Peterborough. "There were a good many passengers, and about a dozen persons, including the Mayor, patronised the line by taking return tickets to Wisbech St Mary and other places, returning at 9.43. There are three trains each way per day from Wisbech ... to Peterborough at 8.48, 2.38 and 6.48 ... to Sutton Bridge at 9.43, 12.33 and 7.43."

The summary shows trains operating more than one day per week.

	Weekdays	Sundays
1870	4	-
1890	8	-
1910	8	-
1930	6	-
1950	8	1

In December 1920 passenger services from Wisbech comprised six weekday trains to South Lynn, and just five to Peterborough. The 3pm from Cromer, which left Wisbech at 5.44pm, included through carriages for London King's Cross, where they arrived at 8.40pm. The July 1936 timetable shows eight weekday Peterborough trains, the first leaving Wisbech at 8am, arriving home on the last train at 8.13pm. Six trains for Sutton Bridge and South Lynn began with the 7.25am, returning home to the 'Midland' station in Wisbech by 6.52pm, or 9.45pm on Saturdays.

A popular feature on this route were afternoon or evening excursion trains to London for exhibitions and the theatre. M&GN handbills advertised a Half-Day Trip to London on Wednesday 15th April 1936, for a 3rd class Return fare of 5/6d. Leaving King's Lynn at 11am, with stops at Sutton Bridge (11.24) Wisbech (11.40) Wisbech St Mary (11.45) and Murrow (11.51), the train arrived in London King's Cross at 2.09pm. A midnight departure allowed plenty of time to visit the Ideal Homes Exhibition at Olympia.

Then in 1950, summer Sunday excursion trains to Hunstanton were introduced, the first advertised Sunday services on the Wisbech M&GN branch since the line opened in 1866! The following year British Railways were advertising evening trips to Peterborough for 3/- from Sutton Bridge, or 2/3d from Wisbech. On Wednesdays and Saturday in January 1951, day excursions to London cost 19/11d from Tydd, and 18/4d from Murrow.

The last M&GN line passenger train for Wisbech, the 8.37pm to Melton Constable, left Peterborough North on Saturday 28th February 1959. After pausing for handshakes and photographs at Peterborough, Murrow, and an unscheduled stop at Wisbech St Mary the train, packed with passengers and enthusiasts, arrived at Wisbech North almost 10 minutes late. As the train left for Sutton Bridge, Porter Ernie Shinkin turned out the gaslamps and locked the station doors for the last time.

December 1870

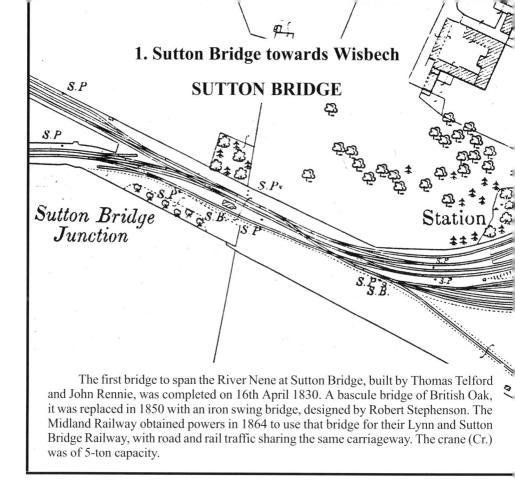

1. Sutton Bridge towards Wisbech

SUTTON BRIDGE

S.P

S.P

Sutton Bridge
Junction

Station

Sutton Bridge Junction

The first bridge to span the River Nene at Sutton Bridge, built by Thomas Telford and John Rennie, was completed on 16th April 1830. A bascule bridge of British Oak, it was replaced in 1850 with an iron swing bridge, designed by Robert Stephenson. The Midland Railway obtained powers in 1864 to use that bridge for their Lynn and Sutton Bridge Railway, with road and rail traffic sharing the same carriageway. The crane (Cr.) was of 5-ton capacity.

1. This second swing bridge, 110ft upstream from the first, opened on 18th July 1897. The 165ft 6in central swing span weighed in at about 750 tons, double that of the first iron bridge. The bridge had two 15ft carriageways to separate road and rail traffic, with a steep outside staircase to the control cabin. (Lens of Sutton)

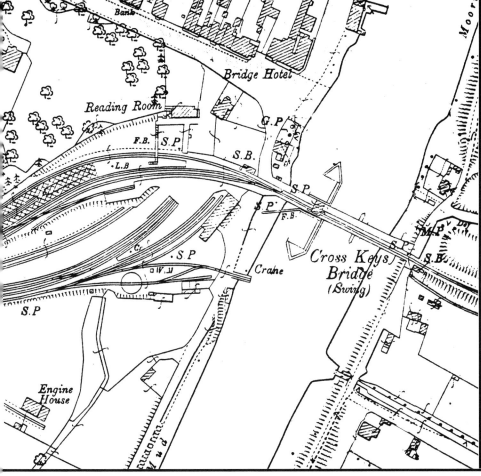

2. The *Prima*, from the German Baltic port of Flensburg, has left Wisbech on the afternoon high tide and negotiates Cross Keys Bridge circa 1925. A smell "as though someone had just been sick" in the control cabin derived from the 20% glycerine solution which acted as the hydraulics system antifreeze and lubricant. In the 1930s, naturalist and painter Peter Scott lived in Sutton Bridge East lighthouse, downstream from the bridge. (H.Coates/A.C.Ingram coll.)

3. Class 4 2-6-0 no. 43091 hauls a South Lynn to Peterborough North train off the bridge and into the station, passing Sutton Bridge Station signal-box, on Tuesday 19th August 1958. From this footbridge vantage point Sutton Bridge East box can be seen to the left of the goods shed. In 1960 the railway track over the bridge was covered with sleepers to form a second roadway, replaced by a permanent carriageway in 1963. (E.Woods)

4. This third station, opened in 1897, was built to allow alignment with the second swing bridge, the older buildings being retained as offices. A massive timber station nameboard facing the Up platform emphasised the importance of this junction. The 1891 census reveals a parish population of just 180. (Lens of Sutton)

February 1890

PETERBRO', WISBECH, SUTTON BRIDGE, and LYNN.—Midland and Great Northern Joint.

Min. from Peterbro'	New Street Sta.	mrn	mrn	mrn	aft		aft	mrn	aft	aft	aft	aft	aft		From Wells, &c., p.129.	mrn	mrn	mrn	mrn	aft	aft	aft	aft	aft		aft	aft
	282 BIRMINGHAM dp				8 5		1112						2 45		Lynn ....dep	7 10	8 40	9 35	1020	12 5	1 52	1 53	3 40	4 52		5 50	6 58
	DERBY 265.. "	6 0		8 49		1142						3 40		South Lynn	7 15	8 45	9 45	1025	1217	1 10	2 2	3 40	5 3		5 55	7 3
	LEICESTER .. "	7 30		9 32		1250						4 35		Clenchwarton.......	7 22	f		1052	Sig.	Sig.	f	3 52			6 2	
	154 LONDON (K.C.) "	3 15		7 40		1015		1 30	2 c0	2 c0		5 c30		Terrington	7 27	8 55	9 53	1056	1229	1 20	2 29	3 57			6 7	7 11
	Peterbro'(G.E.) dep		9 15		1150		3 2				6 55			Walpole.............	7 33	f		1041		Sig.	f	Sig.			6 13	Sig.
	" (Gt. North.) "	6 55	9 20		1157		3 9	3 45	4 49		7 5			Sutton Bridge { arr	7 39	9 3	10 1	1046	1236	1 31	2 37	4 5	5 15		6 19	7 11
6	Eye Green	7 6	9 31		1210		3 20		5 0		7 16			{ dep	7 50	9 4		1047	1237		2 33	5 19	6 21		6 30	
9½	Thorney	7 13	9 39		1218		3 27		5 7		7 23			Tydd	7 56			1053			2 44				6 37	
11½	Wryde........ [153 Sig.		9 45		1224	Sig.			5 13		7 29			Ferry...............	8 2			1059			Sig.				6 41	
15½	Murrow 172, 173,	7 25	9 53		1232	8 38			5 21		7 37			Wisbech* 128	8 12	9 20		11 7	1212		2 53		5 34	6 28	6 53	
18½	Wisbech St. Mary...		10 0		1240	Sig.		Sig.			7 44			Wisbech St. Mary ..	8 18	f		1113			3 1				7 1	
20½	Wisbech * 128	7 34	10 6		1247		3 47	4 18	5 31		7 49			Murrow 172, 173, 153	8 25	9 30		112 l	2	3 8				7 8	
23½	Ferry	Sig.	1014		Sig.		Sig.		5 33		7 57			Wryde	8 33	f		1127			3 18				7 16	
25½	Tydd		1020		1 1		4 0		5 45		8 3			Thorney..[and above	8 39	9 40		1133	1 11		3 25			b	7 23	
28½	Sutton Bridge { arr	7 48	1025		1 6		4 6	4 32	5 50		8 8			Eye Green (154, 172,	8 46	9 46		1139	l 17		3 36		g		7 29	
	159 { dep	7 49	9 19	102 3	1215	1 7	4 45	4 7	33		6 20	8 9 9 5		Peterbro' (G.N.) 157,	8 55	9 58		1150	1 30		3 48		6 7	7 12	7 42	
31	Walpole		Sig.	1032	1220	1 14	Sig.	ʃ			6 27	8 16 d		" (G. E.) 130		10 2		1155			3 53		6 12	7 16	7 45	
33	Torrington	7 58	9 30	1036	1226	1 20	3 57	4 18			6 33	8 22 9 14		157 LONDON (K. C.) arr	11 e9	1145		1 55	3 20		5 45		7 55	9 20	9 20	
34½	Clenchwarton......		Tu.	1042	1234	1 24	Sig.	a			6 37	a Sig.		LEICESTER ... "		1119	12 0		1 43		6 40			9 42	9 42	
37½	South Lynn 122 ..	8 5	9 41	1049	1241	1 31	4 7	4 27	4 48		6 43	8 30 9 22		260 DERBY (Sta. St.) "	1232	1254		2 50			7 45			1055	1055	
39½	Lynn 123, 129..arr	8 10	9 46	1055	1247	1 38	4 15	4 32	4 55		6 52	8 38 9 28		262 BIRMINGHAM .. "	1240			3 2			8 24			2 7	2 7	

a Stops when required to set down from Wisbech and Stations West thereof.   b Stops when required to set down from beyond Lynn, and take up for Grantham and North thereof.   c Slips carriage at Peterboro'.   d Stops to set down from Stations North of Sutton Bridge.   e Arrives at 10 40 mrn. on Mondays.

5. Class 4F 0-6-0 nos. 43954 and 44231 sweep into Sutton Bridge with the 11.10am Yarmouth Beach to Leicester train on Saturday 30th August 1958. Heading west past Sutton Bridge Junction the M&GN carried traffic to Spalding and Bourne, before joining the Midland line at Little Bytham Junction. Following the withdrawal of passenger services in 1959, goods trains continued working between Sutton Bridge and Spalding. (H.Ballantyne)

6. The 200 yard island station platform, built on an "S" bend with a 1 in 110 gradient, was photographed on Saturday 23rd August 1958. Sutton Bridge goods yard (left) stood on the old Norwich & Spalding Railway station alignment. Beyond these sidings the RAF established an armament training camp at Wingland Airfield. After bombing practice over The Wash, aircraft were refuelled and crew debriefed before returning to their home bases. (John Langford)

7. The Wisbech branch was generally regarded as a main line, due to the importance of Peterborough as a railway centre. Class 4 no. 43145 departs with a Yarmouth Beach to Wisbech and Peterborough train on Saturday 28th February 1959, the last day of passenger services. Six years later the last goods train left Sutton Bridge on Friday 2nd April 1965. (A.E.Bennett)

8. A Down train from Peterborough passes Sutton Bridge Junction signal box, 300 yards west of Sutton Bridge station, with the Swing Bridge Hydraulic "Tower" to its right. A visit to this Tower in the 1970s revealed racks of spanners stamped M&GN, and a mahogany-cased M&GN clock on the wall. By 1997 it stood derelict and up for sale. (H.P.White/A.Mott)

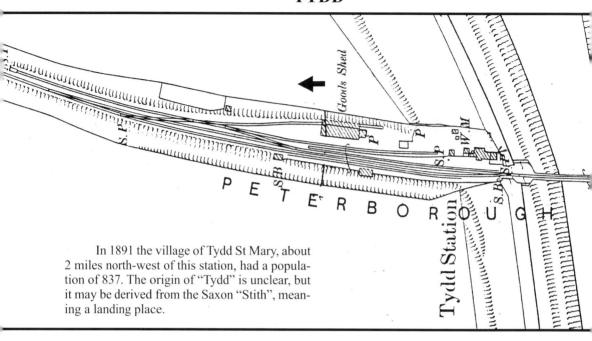

In 1891 the village of Tydd St Mary, about 2 miles north-west of this station, had a population of 837. The origin of "Tydd" is unclear, but it may be derived from the Saxon "Stith", meaning a landing place.

9. Tydd station is seen from the south, following the addition of a passing loop and timber Down platform in 1896. Gates for this level crossing on the Sutton Bridge road were operated from the wooden gate cabin on the left. The wooden goods shed at Tydd was gutted by fire on Saturday 1st February 1947, destroying several wagons and thousands of empty sacks. (Lens of Sutton)

10. No. 43088 prepares to depart on 31st August 1958 with the 9.55am Sundays Only service from Murrow East to Hunstanton. This popular holiday destination has now lost its seafront station, the GER Sandringham Hotel and an 800ft long pier with a miniature railway. An unusual spectacle for visitors to that East Coast resort are sunsets over the sea. (H.Ballantyne)

11. Tydd Up platform had retained its enamel station nameboard, for in the 1920s reinforced concrete replaced many earlier wooden and enamel examples on the M&GN. Tydd and Ferry were the only stations on this branch to lose their goods facilities in 1959, although Tydd had a temporary Parcels Depot at Tydd Gote pub until about 1962. (E.Woods)

12. The North Level Main Drain, constructed between 1831 and 1834, entered the River Nene at Gunthorpe Sluice just beyond M&GN bridge no. 27. On Saturday 4th October 1958 class 4MT no. 43094 crosses this bridge, heading towards Peterborough. Designed by H.G.Ivatt and introduced in 1947, these locomotives worked most passenger and goods trains on this branch in the 1950s. (F.Church/E.B.E.G.)

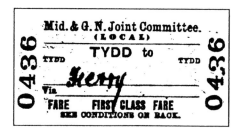

Mid. & G. N. Joint Committee.
(LOCAL)
TYDD to
TYDD   TYDD
Via   Kerry
FARE   FIRST CLASS FARE
SEE CONDITIONS ON BACK.
0436   0436

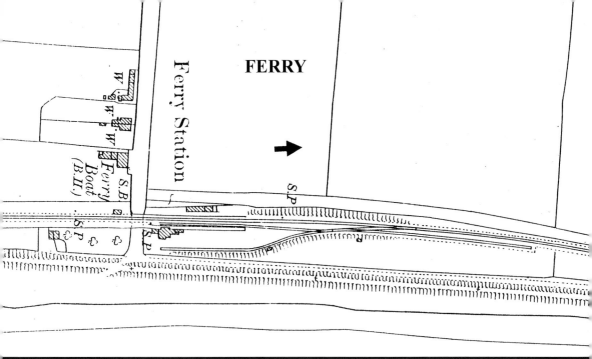

FERRY

Ferry station, Cambridgeshire lay within the Norfolk parish and village of West Walton, one mile to the east. A ferry boat sailed across the tidal River Nene to the Ferry Boat Inn. Records for 1812 in St Mary's Church, West Walton include the following entry: "One year's salary paid to William Holman for ferrying Rev Mair and others over Walton Dam £1.10s.0d".

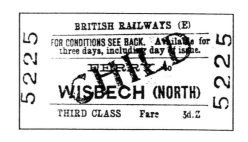

13. A timber waiting room alongside the only single-platform station on the branch, this is Ferry on Saturday 4th October 1958. It was also the only goods yard between Peterborough and Sutton Bridge with no facilities for handling livestock. Bradshaw's timetable for December 1920 records four weekday passenger trains to Sutton Bridge and three to Peterborough. (F.Church/E.B.E.G.)

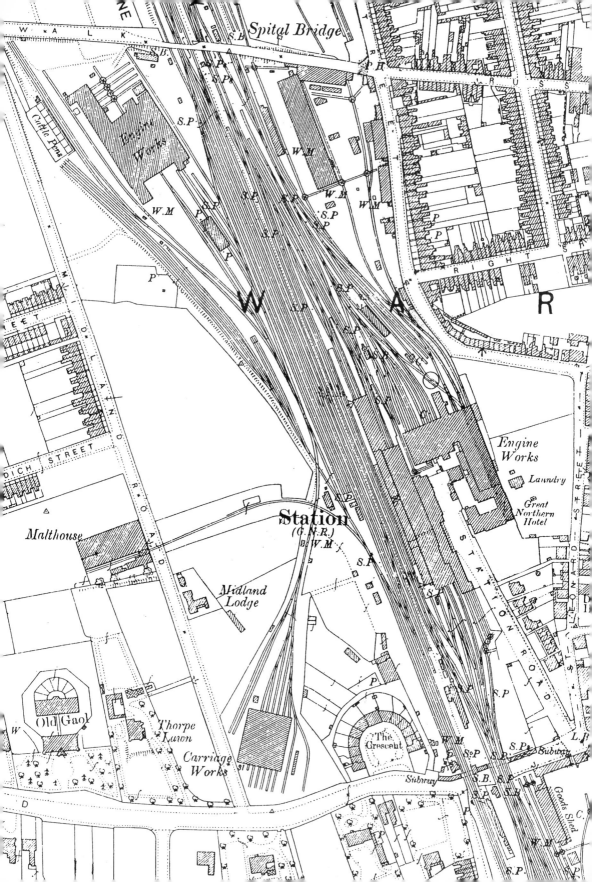

2. Peterborough towards Wisbech

PETERBOROUGH NORTH

The Peterborough (GNR) station, designed by Henry Goddard of Lincoln, opened officially on Monday 5th August 1850. The Midland Railway Engine Works, opened in May 1872, stand beside Spital Bridge. The station was renamed Peterborough North on 1st October 1923. The scale is 20ins to 1 mile.

14. The Norman cathedral of St Peter has dominated Peterborough's skyline since the 12th century. At the northern end of platform 3 in 1958 stands class A3 no. 60055 Woolwinder with a down express, whilst at platform 6 class B1 no. 61207 heads a north-bound stopping train. M&GN services used both through and bay platforms. (A.V.Fincham/A.C.Ingram)

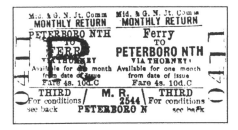

15. Sparrows chirp in the eaves during a lull in traffic on a sunny Sunday lunchtime. Soon the platforms will echo to the exhaust of a locomotive, the ring of a wheeltapper's hammer, and the rhythm of carriage wheels over an uneven rail joint. At the north end of platform 3 a waiting room, complete with large windows and a coal fire, sheltered trainspotters from wind and rain. (A.V.Fincham/A.C.Ingram)

17. In the 1930s pre-grouping carriage stock of LNWR, MR, NER and GER origin were transferred to the M&GN. Class 4MT no. 43058, with an LNWR corridor third marshalled behind, pulls away from platform 3 on Friday 11th May 1951, heading for Wisbech and King's Lynn. The tall signals alerted spotters to the imminent arrival of a down train at Platform 2. (M.N.Bland)

16. The GNR and M&GN introduced a regular 3pm King's Cross to Cromer service in 1894. Bradshaw's July 1936 timetable shows departure from Peterborough at 4.45pm, with stops at Thorney (4.58), Wisbech (5.16), and Sutton Bridge (5.28) on the Wisbech branch, before arriving in Cromer Beach station at 7.36pm. LNER class D53 no. 050 stands at Platform 3 with the 3pm from London on Friday 20th May 1938. This service ended in September 1939 with the outbreak of war. (H.C.Casserley)

←——————

18. In May 1982 British Rail introduced a Rail Link coach service between Peterborough, Wisbech and King's Lynn, seen here outside the Great Northern Hotel on Saturday 9th July 1983. Following BR's decision to withdraw the service in 1993, Eastern Counties Omnibus Co. extended their X94 Excel Service to include stops at Peterborough and King's Lynn rail stations. (J.H.Price)

SPITAL BRIDGE

19. The Peterborough allocation of M&GN locomotives, originally housed in the GER shed at Peterborough East, was transferred to Spital Bridge in 1872. The LNER took over responsibility for M&GN services in October 1936, and transferred 11 locomotives back to Peterborough East. A year later they moved to New England shed, but Spital Bridge, seen here in 1958, continued to service Joint line locomotives until closure.
(A.V.Fincham/A.C.Ingram)

20. In August 1950 Spital Bridge was transferred to the Eastern Region under the control of New England, the Midland Region 16B shedcode changing to 35C. This 1957 photograph reveals an allocation of LMS, LNER and BR Standard classes. In February 1958, two years before closure, Cambridge shed assumed responsibility, which required another code change, this time to 31F. (A.V.Fincham/A.C.Ingram)

21. M&GN class C no. 18, with a mixed train of GNR coaches and cattle wagons, approaches Peterborough station circa 1900. GNR 0-6-0T no. 907, later LNER class J54, shunts in Westwood Yard beside the GN main line. M&GN services worked over this line from Peterborough North, crossing over to the Midland at Westwood Junction, before reaching M&GN territory at Wisbech Junction. (HMRS/ Richard Hilton coll.)

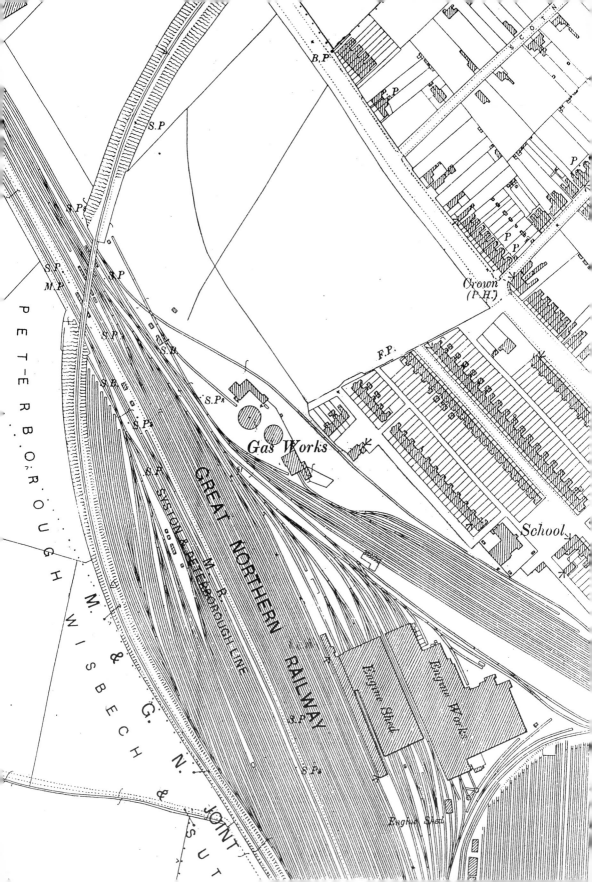

NEW ENGLAND

22. No. 43068 with a Wisbech-bound train crosses the MR and GNR lines on M&GN bridge no. 1, officially called New England Bridge. Although known to railwaymen as Crab Bridge, enthusiasts and local residents used the nickname Rhubarb Bridge. This name originated after soil, imported for the railway and Lincoln Road bridge embankments, produced a fine crop of leafy stems. A modern concrete bridge at this same spot, carrying the A47 trunk road, still bears the name Rhubarb. (H.Cooke/A.C.Ingram)

This map is to the north of the previous and is at the same scale. The Great Northern Railway's main locomotive shed and works at New England were situated one mile north of Peterborough station. Its allocation of 185 locomotives in 1912 increased to 213, representing 21 classes, by 1950. The M&GN route curves over the GNR main line.

DOGSTHORPE SIDING

The Down sidings at Dogsthorpe were provided for the marshalling and loading of wagons from the adjacent brickworks. Additional sidings on the Up side were opened on 21st July 1943 to serve a new 5,000 ton capacity grain silo for the Ministry of Food.

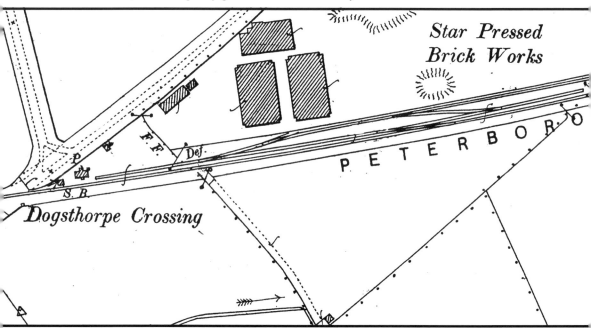

23. Dogsthorpe Siding signal box beside Welland Road level crossing on Thursday 3rd August 1961. Following closure of the M&GN as a through route in February 1959, and demolition of Rhubarb Bridge in October 1961, the western section terminated at Dogsthorpe. This box closed on 9th September 1962 but brick traffic continued until 18th April 1966, gaining access to the national network via a connecting spur at Murrow, opened on 17th December 1960. (J.Watling)

EYE GREEN

The Northamptonshire village of Eye, three miles north-east of Peterborough, was six miles distant by train according to Bradshaw's timetable. The station, originally named Eye, became Eye Green (for Crowland) on 1st October 1875. The Down waiting shelter, installed in 1897, had previously stood on the Up platform at Sheringham. The Northam Brick Works sidings opened on 1st March 1898. There was a one-ton crane in the goods shed.

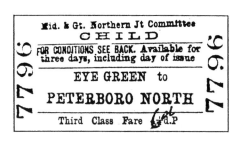

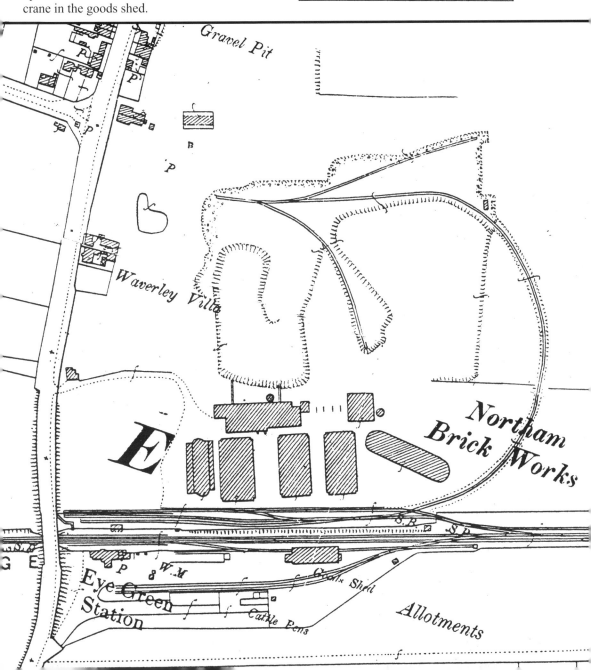

PETERBRO', MARCH, WISBECH, and LYNN.—Great Eastern.

Miles	Down.	mrn		mrn		mrn	mrn	mrn	aft		aft	aft	aft	aft	aft	aft	aft	aft		Sundays
																				aft aft
	Peterbro' ....dep.	7 14				8 58	9 30	11 36	1 5		2 52	3 20	4 25	4 58	7 5	7 5	10 58			4 40 10 58
14	March .... "	7 45	9 0		9 28	9 55	12 15	1 40		3 30	4 54	49	5 26	7 33	8 35	1 10		5 3 10
22	Wisbech* .... "	8 2	9 27		9 47		12 42	1 53	3 0	47	4 18	5 2	5 50	7 46	8 51	1 26		1 26
24	Emneth	8 8	9 33		9 53		12 48		3 6	53		6 2		8 57				
25	Smeeth Road	8 12	9 37		9 57	12 52		3 10	57		6 6	h	9 1				
27	Middle Drove	8 16	9 41		10 1	12 56		3 14	4 1		6 10		9 5				
33	Magdalen Road (see above).	8 25	9 50		1012	1 6		3 23	4 10		6 19		9 14	1 46		6 6 1 46
39	Lynn 391, 392 & above arr.	8 35	10 0		1023	11 13	1 17	2 19	3 35	4 20	4 45	28	6 29	8 11	9 24	2 0		6 20 2 0
Mls	Up.	mrn	mrn	mrn	mrn		aft	aft	aft	aft	aft		aft	aft			aft
—	Lynn ....dep.	7 35	8 47	10 6	12 12		2 0	4 27	5 40	7 21		7 53	10 30				10 30
6	Magdalen Road	7 46	8 58			12 30	2 11	4 37		7 31		8 7	10 43				10 43
12	Middle Drove	7 56	9 8			12 39	2 20	4 46		7 40		8 16				
14	Smeeth Road	8 0	9 12			12 43	2 24	4 50		7 44		8 20				
15	Emneth	8 8	9 16			12 49	2 28	4 55		7 51		8 25				
17	Wisbech * 390 ......arr.	8 13	9 21	1030	1236		12 54	2 35	4 59	6 4	7 56		8 30	11 2			11 2
25	March 388 .... "		9 34	1043	1248		2 50	5 19	6 17	8 12		8 48	1118				1118
39	Peterbro' .... "		10 5	1122	1 25		3 22	5 52	6 42	8 48		9 23	1 43				1 43

h Stops at 7 52 aft. on Mondays to set down from London. * About ¾ mile to Midland Station.

July 1910

24. The Up platform at Eye Green, seen here on Thursday 3rd August 1961, was a mirror image of the station building at Thorney. Passenger traffic, which had always been light at Eye, ceased at the intermediate stations between Peterborough and Murrow on 2nd December 1957. The village now has regular bus services to Crowland, Spalding, Peterborough and Wisbech. (J.Watling)

25. Most stations on the M&GN had cattle docks, with special trains working to Wisbech for the Thursday market. This water tank, photographed on Thursday 3rd August 1961, may have been used to provide drinking water for livestock, and wash down the pens after use to prevent disease. (J.Watling)

26. Brickmaking has been a major industry in the Peterborough area for over 100 years. Local yards, such as Northam on the right, provided Eye with much of its employment, but a northerly wind blew pungent fumes into the village. The chimneys have now gone and the A47 trunk road has been laid on this trackbed from Eye Green towards Rhubarb Bridge. (M.Back)

THORNEY

27. The line from Thorney to Eye Green, originally single track, was doubled on 27th February 1900. This is a view from Station Road level crossing, on the B1040 to Crowland, looking west towards Peterborough around 1937. In the 1930s this area's chief crops were wheat, oats and potatoes, with some grazing pastures. (Stations UK)

In 1634 the whole parish of Thorney, on the north-west border of Cambridgeshire, was granted by the Crown to Francis, 4th Earl of Bedford. He devised a scheme which, under the direction of Dutch drainage engineer Cornelius Vermuyden, transformed about 2,000 square acres of wasteland into some of the most fertile land in England. The goods shed crane was of 30 cwt capacity.

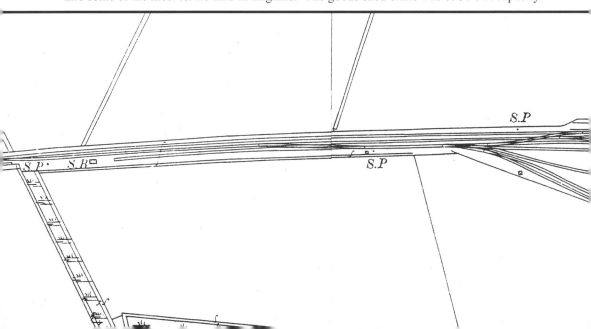

28. Passenger traffic ceased on 2nd December 1957, but the goods yard remained open until 28th December 1964. The brick goods shed in picture no. 27 has been demolished, but the large wooden grain warehouse, built in 1892, and station buildings were still intact when photographed in August 1961. (J.Watling)

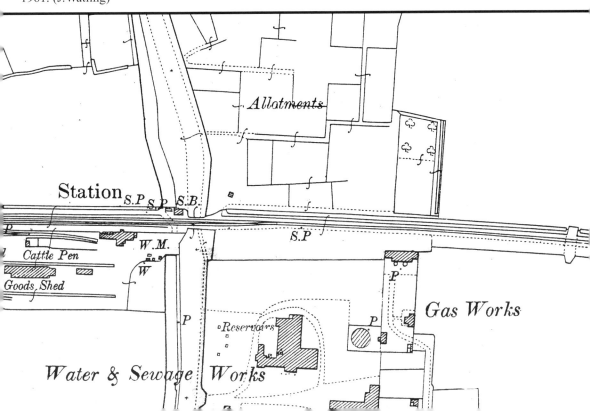

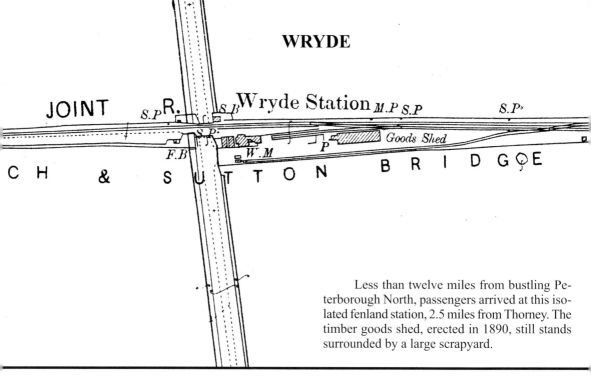

WRYDE

JOINT   *S.P* **R.**   *S.B* Wryde Station *M.P* *S.P*   *S.P*ˢ

S.P.

F.B   *W.M*   *P*   Goods Shed

C H   &   S U T T O N   B R I D G E

Less than twelve miles from bustling Peterborough North, passengers arrived at this isolated fenland station, 2.5 miles from Thorney. The timber goods shed, erected in 1890, still stands surrounded by a large scrapyard.

29. Wryde, in common with most stations on this branch, gained much of its revenue from handling agricultural traffic. In July 1936 just four Peterborough and four Wisbech weekday passenger trains stopped here. This 1937 photograph includes the Up platform signal box, which replaced the earlier box on 26th June 1906, when a passing loop was laid through the station. (Stations UK)

30. The wooden booking office, complete with platform clock, and waiting room appear to have been an afterthought. Class WD 2-8-0 no. 90175, allocated to 40B Immingham, with an Up goods train on Thursday 3rd August 1961. The M&GN somersault home signal indicates line clear, yet there is no tablet in the adjacent apparatus. (J.Watling)

31. A tablet pouch now hangs on the Whitaker automatic apparatus. Wryde stood approximately mid-way on the six-mile stretch of single track between Thorney and Murrow. An oil lamp, with the station name in blue letters on a white background, illuminated the apparatus and boarded foot crossing. (J.Watling)

32. An agricultural light railway ran west from Wryde station to serve the fertile Bedford Level. The regular horse traction has given way to manpower by 1932. This system was in regular use during WWII, but had been abandoned by the early 1950s. Short lengths of 2ft gauge track were still visible in 1997, running into an agricultural shed opposite the station.
(Lilian Ream Exhibition Gallery)

MURROW EAST

33. The timber Up platform building at Murrow was erected in 1901. After nationalisation British Railways added the EAST suffix below the station nameboards, to avoid confusion with nearby Murrow West. Valancing panels from the Down platform canopy had been missing since pre-grouping days. (Stations UK)

34. The GN&GE station, renamed Murrow West on 27th September 1948, closed in 1953. This is the Down platform at Murrow East on its last day of passenger services, Saturday 28th February 1959. Murrow is now served by one return bus to Peterborough every Wednesday and Saturday, and one return bus to Wisbech every Thursday and Saturday. (A.E.Bennett)

35. A group of forty "mourners" arrive back at Murrow on the last 8.37pm from Peterborough, to be greeted by Station Master Stan Carter, and undertaker Martin Henson in his top hat. Earlier, three gentlemen in funeral dress had walked through the crowded train taking last orders for dinner! (Fenland Citizen)

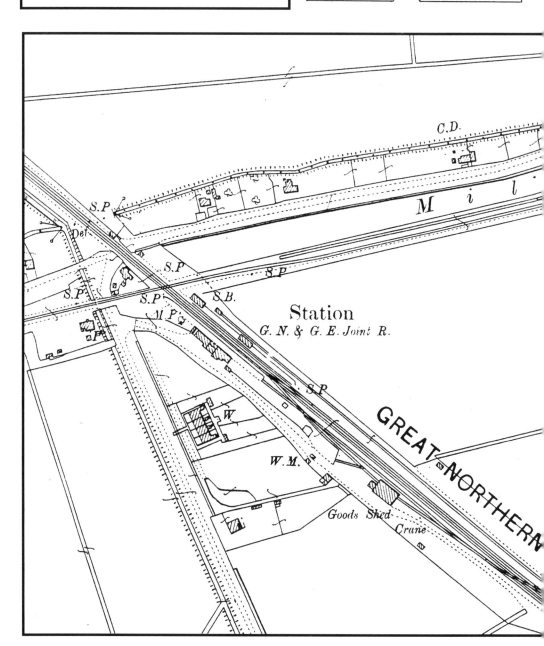

C.D.

M i l

S.P.

Def.

S.P.

S.P

S.P.

S.P.

S.B.

S.P.

M.P.

Station
G. N. & G. E. Joint R.

S.P

W

W.M.

Goods Shed
Crane

GREAT NORTHERN

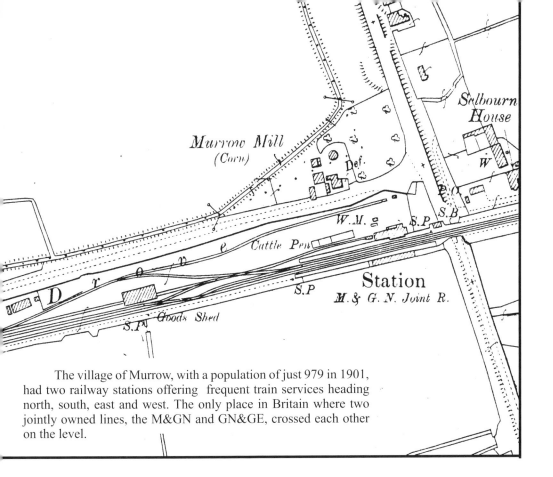

Murrow Mill
(Corn)

Selbourn House

W

Def.

W.M.

S.B

S.P

Cattle Pen

Station

M. & G. N. Joint R.

S.P

D

Goods Shed

S.P

The village of Murrow, with a population of just 979 in 1901, had two railway stations offering frequent train services heading north, south, east and west. The only place in Britain where two jointly owned lines, the M&GN and GN&GE, crossed each other on the level.

WISBECH ST MARY

36. Passenger services through Wisbech St. Mary commenced on 1st August 1866. In the twelve months from February 1900 the M&GN doubled the original single track through all intermediate stations between Peterborough and Wisbech, with the exception of Wryde. We look east towards Wisbech on a sunny winter's afternoon in 1959. (Stations UK)

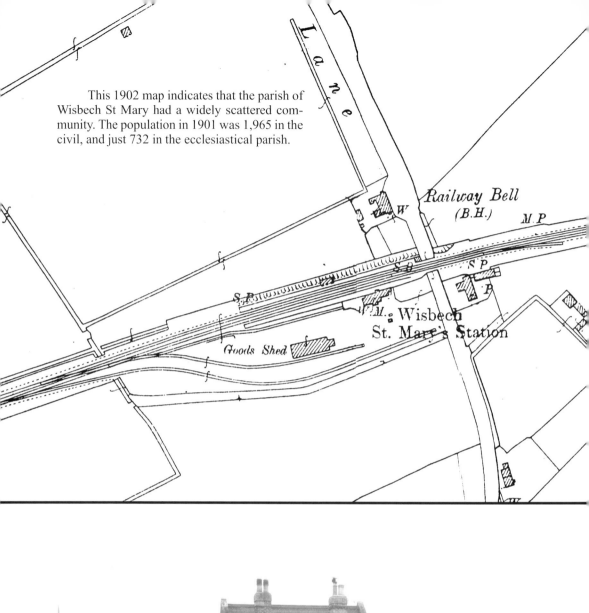

This 1902 map indicates that the parish of Wisbech St Mary had a widely scattered community. The population in 1901 was 1,965 in the civil, and just 732 in the ecclesiastical parish.

Railway Bell (B.H.)

Goods Shed

M.ₑ Wisbech St. Mary's Station

(lower left)
37. The Up platform buildings, almost identical to Thorney station, on a cold winter's day. Originally named Wisbeach St Mary, the spelling of both M&GN and GER station names were altered to Wisbech on 4th May 1877. Critics suggested that this company's initials stood for the Muddle & Go Nowhere Railway. (E.Woods)

38. Station Master A.W.Palmer is pictured in the booking hall at Wisbech St Mary, following his transfer from Hatfield Peverel in August 1956. He had been a Station Master since 1947, and held similar positions at North Kelsey and Whitlingham Junction stations. His predecessor at Wisbech St Mary, Percy Shortland, had been appointed Station Master at Wisbech North. (Lilian Ream Exhibition Gallery)

39. As a 19 year old lad in 1899, Bob Garner had helped to lay track through the village. He was one of a gang of 40 Permanent Way staff, each earning 18 shillings a week. Now in April 1965 he watches as just one crane lifts the M&GN line running through Wisbech St Mary. (Lilian Ream Exhibition Gallery)

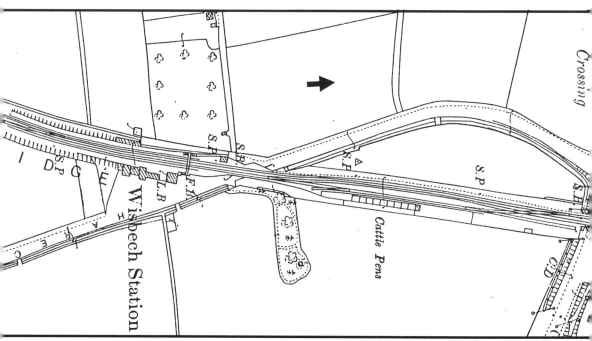

Wisbech North station's design, a large single-storey timber building, was unique to this branch. An office for Station Master Henry Charles Fisher was added to the Up platform in 1892; then in 1903 doors and windows were fitted to the previously open waiting areas on both platforms. The station area was cleared in March 1982 for housing, now called Cricketers Way.

40. M&GN class C no. 76, allocated to Spital Bridge shed, with a train from Peterborough on Saturday 27th April 1935. Designed by S.W.Johnson, this locomotive worked both goods and passenger traffic on the M&GN from entering traffic in October 1899 until withdrawal by the LNER in July 1943. (H.C.Casserley)

41. In April 1934 the Wisbech M&GN St John Ambulance team gained the Elgood cup in keen competition. Photographed on the Up platform are Back row: Signalman J.S.Bailey, C.F.Allbrow, E.R.Barrett (reserve), Booking Clerk Matthew Crosby. Front row: Station Master W.Curzon, A.R.Osborn (captain), F.E.Fernie. This followed the winning example of other railway teams, as Tydd M&GN staff had won the cup in 1929. (Lilian Ream Exhibition Gallery)

42. The first batch of evacuees from London arrive in Wisbech on Friday 1st September 1939. They are being subjected to a cursory medical inspection on the platform before leaving for their new homes. The naturalist Professor David Bellamy first came to Wisbech as an evacuee, and he has loved The Fens ever since. (G.Drew coll.)

43. The Royal Train, conveying HM The Queen, HRH The Duke of Edinburgh, and their two children, stops for water at 10.45am on Monday 9th February 1953. Hauled by class B2 no. 61671 ROYAL SOVEREIGN, the train traversed the M&GN route as the disastrous East Coast Floods had cut the line between Lynn and Downham. (Lilian Ream Exhibition Gallery)

44. A mid-day lull on Saturday 9th July 1955, looking towards Sutton Bridge. Following the line's closure in 1964, windows and door frames from the Down waiting room were incorporated into a nearby garden shed. In the 1970s a WISBECH seat nameplate was discovered in a local cycle repair workshop - being used as a tortoise-stove poker. (E.Course)

45. Harecroft Road gates, operated by a large wheel in the signal-box, opening for road traffic after the passage of a Down train on Saturday 9th July 1955. Across the road another gate leads to livestock pens, with the fenced approaches providing a resting place for animals prior to loading. (E.Course)

46. Signalman and Methodist local preacher Stephen J Ludlow at work in Wisbech North signal-box. He retired on 31st January 1953 after nearly 50 years of railway service. Note the large brass plate down the side of each lever; he selects CONTROLS HAND GATES DOWN SIDE. This box was offered for sale by British Railways in the 1960s for the princely sum of £9.10s.0d. (Lilian Ream Exhibition Gallery

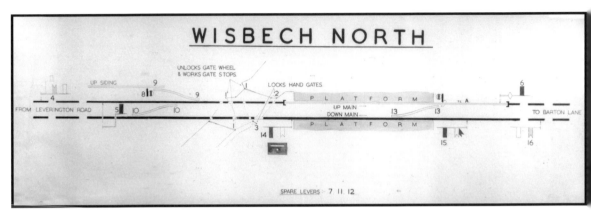

WISBECH NORTH

UNLOCKS GATE WHEEL
& WORKS GATE STOPS

LOCKS HAND GATES

UP SIDING

FROM LEVERINGTON ROAD

PLATFORM

UP MAIN
DOWN MAIN

PLATFORM

TO BARTON LANE

SPARE LEVERS — 7 11 12

47. Station Master Percy Shortland greets members of the Loco Spotters' Club on Saturday 4th October 1958. Railway publisher Ian Allan accompanied these enthusiasts on the first diesel train to run between Peterborough and Sutton Bridge. Another special, organised by the M&GN Preservation Society, worked over the remaining M&GN lines, including the Murrow to Wisbech North section, in 1961. (Lilian Ream Exhibition Gallery)

48. Driver Watts and Fireman Willet prepare to leave Wisbech with the 8.37pm from Peterborough on Saturday 28th February 1959. Mr Shortland, along with local residents, bids farewell to this last M&GN passenger train. Guard F.R.Bushell gave the right-away, then rockets soared into the air, and fog detonators exploded, as no. 43145 headed for Sutton Bridge. (Fenland Citizen)

49. The station building stood for another 23 years following closure, with goods traffic working through on the remaining Up line until 1964. The forecourt and Up platform buildings were taken over by Clarke Bros garage, but a crawl through the very dusty loft in 1977 unearthed a large collection of M&GN telegrams and waybills. This photograph on Saturday 20th September 1980 was taken eighteen months before demolition. (A.C.Ingram)

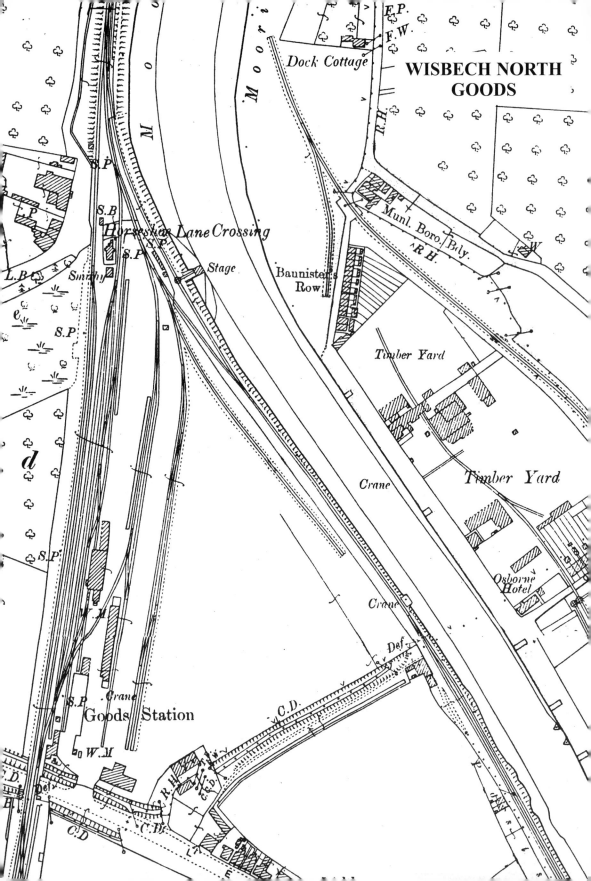

WISBECH NORTH
GOODS

Dock Cottage

F.P.
F.W.

R.H.

Horseshoe Lane Crossing

S.P.

S.B.

S.P.

S.P.

Smithy

Stage

Baunister's
Row

Munl. Boro. Bdy.
R.H.

W

Timber Yard

d

S.P.

Crane

Timber Yard

Osborne
Hotel

W.M.

Crane

Def.

S.P.

Crane

Goods Station

C.D.

W.M.

R.H.

C.D.

D.

Def.

C.D.

C.D.

The original brick offices fronting Leverington Road have been retained, but this once extensive goods yard is now covered with modern storage warehouses. Samuel Smith, the first-known English documentary photographer, lived beside Horseshoe Lane Crossing from 1852 until his death in 1898. This map shows the M&GN line heading north towards Sutton Bridge, with GER harbour branch sidings on the far side of the River Nene. The crane could lift seven tons.

50. In 1896 a total of 4,400 tons of fruit were dispatched from Wisbech M&GN by goods and passenger train. M&GN class C no. 42, built in May 1894, heads towards Peterborough hauling box vans laden with fruit circa 1900. The train is approaching Harecroft Road, with Leverington Road crossing and signal-box in the background, whilst M&GN cattle wagon no. 476 stands alongside the livestock pens.
(Wisbech & Fenland Museum)

51. Leverington Road Crossing signal box stood beside the A1101 to Long Sutton, and was photographed on Saturday 9th May 1964. Seven months later the last Up M&GN goods train, consisting of 43 wagons hauled by D5619, passed this box at 4.15pm on Christmas Eve 1964, with the traditional salvo of fog detonators. (John Langford)

52. Produce from the leading Midland Railway cart is loaded into the same company's vans, for conveyance at passenger train speeds. Between June and September 1894 local farmers consigned 3,908 tons of fruit by goods train from this yard, with a further 230 tons being sent by passenger train. For several weeks between 60 and 91 tons per day were handled by Station Master Fisher's staff, whilst on the busiest day 125 tons were forwarded to market. (Wisbech & Fenland Museum)

54. Here we can enjoy a studio portrait by Lilian Ream of M&GN employee Mr Dent. This dark green corduroy uniform for manual staff was phased out after 1926. Mrs Ream's photographic business closed in 1971, but fortunately around 100,000 glass and film negatives still survive. There is a permanent display of her photographs within the Wisbech Tourist Information Centre. (Lilian Ream Exhibition Gallery)

53. On the right, fruit and vegetables are weighed before loading into Great Northern clerestory ventilated vans. The last Wisbech railway horse "Charlie" retired in December 1947, made redundant by the introduction of motor lorries. In the early 1960s LMS class 8F 2-8-0 locomotives regularly shunted Wisbech North Goods, later replaced by the ubiquitous Brush Type 2 diesels. (Wisbech & Fenland Museum)

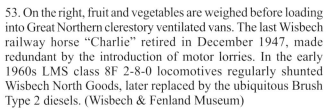

55. The Coal Drop at Horseshoe Corner pre-dates the railway; this primitive example was photographed in 1857. This was later rebuilt by the Midland Railway allowing horse-drawn coal wagons to access the Drop via a turntable, indicated on the map. Six men were usually employed in emptying coal into a sailing ship's hold, but following a fall in demand the Drop was withdrawn from service in February 1904. (Lilian Ream Exhibition Gallery)

56. Here is an aerial view of Wisbech North Goods looking south around 1958, with the M&GN harbour branch leaving Horse Shoe Lane Junction. Wooden stumps in the riverbank are the rotting foundations of the Coal Drop. Trade at Wisbech Port had already been in decline when a new port, Sutton Bridge, received its first vessel on Friday 28th August 1987. In 1996 only 46 vessels berthed at Wisbech, compared with 560 arriving at Sutton Bridge. (Wisbech & Fenland Museum)

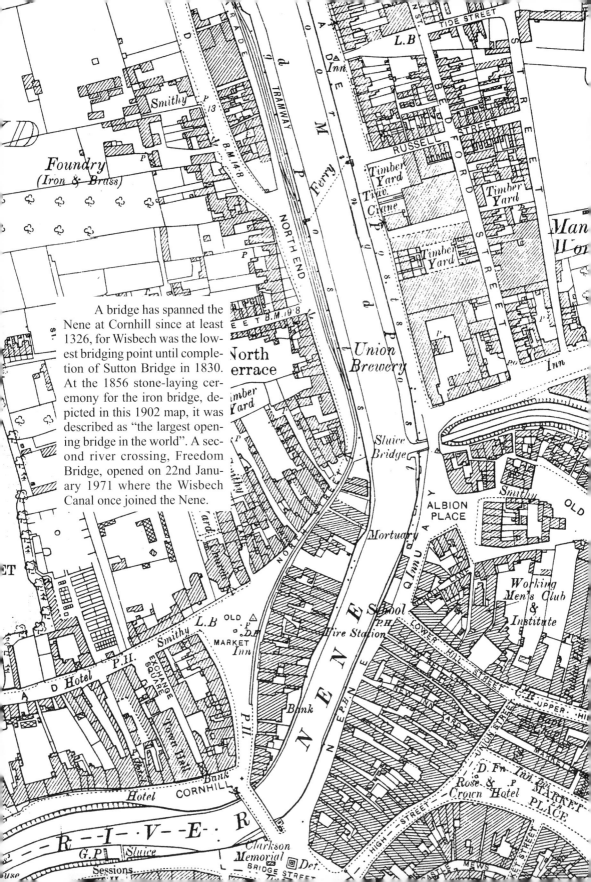

A bridge has spanned the Nene at Cornhill since at least 1326, for Wisbech was the lowest bridging point until completion of Sutton Bridge in 1830. At the 1856 stone-laying ceremony for the iron bridge, depicted in this 1902 map, it was described as "the largest opening bridge in the world". A second river crossing, Freedom Bridge, opened on 22nd January 1971 where the Wisbech Canal once joined the Nene.

WISBECH NORTH HARBOUR BRANCH

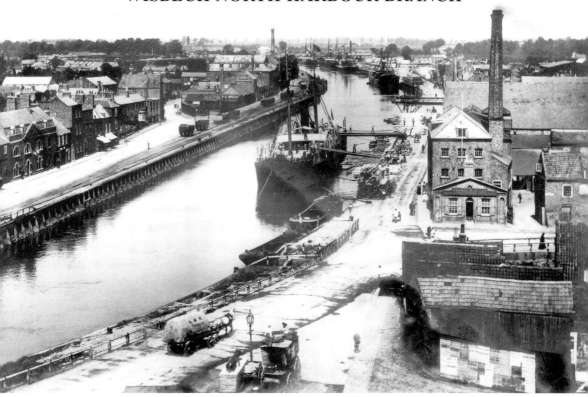

57. The southern end of Wisbech Port is seen from the Working Men's Institute clock tower. From this 96ft high vantage point a carillon still chimes the quarters and plays a tune every two hours. Loose wagons stand alongside the Midland Railway Wharf and Sack Depot on the west bank, while vast quantities of timber are unloaded by dockers and English Bros travelling crane along Nene Parade. (Lilian Ream Exhibition Gallery)

58. The first vessel carrying foreign timber arrived at Wisbech in 1824. Before the quays were piled in 1854, horses hauled wood up the muddy river bank. Dockers unload 400 tons of timber from the *Gisela Flint*, registered in the Sweden port of Karlsham, onto new 15T wagons in April 1963. (Lilian Ream Exhibition Gallery)

59. Fruit, potato, grain and seed warehouses on the left were serviced by river, road, and the harbour branch. Tonnage handled at Wisbech Port rose from 63,180 tons in 1830, to 167,442 tons by 1847, as Wisbech became the largest corn-shipping port in the country. By the early 1950s a Fordson Muirhead tractor-bulldozer had replaced the shunting horse on this branch. Parked vehicles straddle the line as it leaves the quayside to negotiate North Street on Tuesday 10th December 1958. (Lilian Ream Exhibition Gallery)

60. The harbour branch terminated outside Barclays Bank in the Old Market. A lamp standard notice warns "No steam engine to be parked here". Wisbech Octagon Church, opened in 1831 as a Chapel of Ease, complemented the Georgian architecture surrounding this busy market until 1952. Distinguished historian Sir Nicholas Pevsner records in his Buildings of England that "The Octagon Church, to the disgrace of Wisbech, has been demolished". (H.Coates/G.Drew coll.)

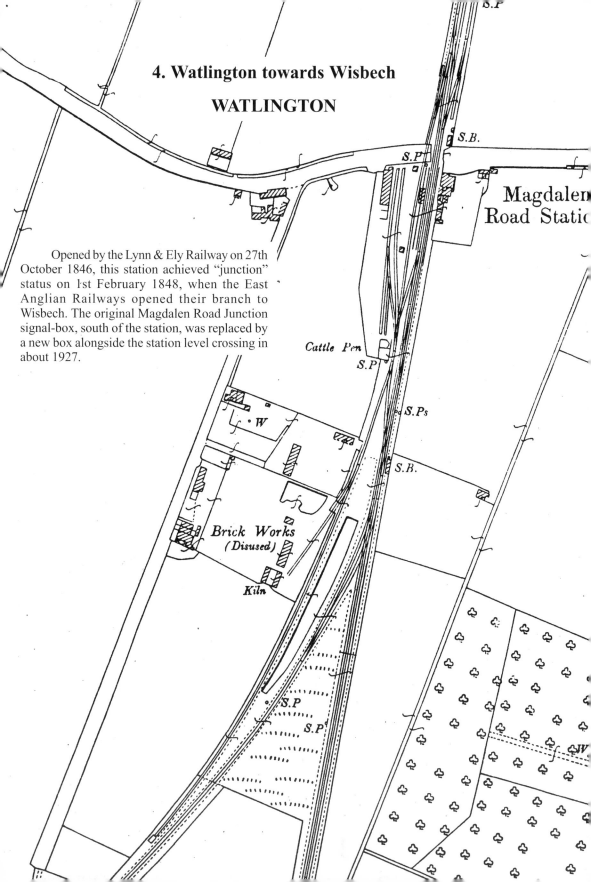

4. Watlington towards Wisbech

WATLINGTON

S.B.

S.P

Magdalen
Road Station

Opened by the Lynn & Ely Railway on 27th October 1846, this station achieved "junction" status on 1st February 1848, when the East Anglian Railways opened their branch to Wisbech. The original Magdalen Road Junction signal-box, south of the station, was replaced by a new box alongside the station level crossing in about 1927.

Cattle Pen

S.P

S.Ps

S.B.

· *W*

Brick Works
(Disused)

Kiln

S.P

S.P

W

61. Up trains for the Wisbech branch obtained a single-line tablet from apparatus beside the signal-box. A Book Room on the Up platform, seen here on Tuesday 16th October 1962, contained many treasures for the railway collector. Waybills, luggage labels, pre-grouping ledgers - even an enamel station nameplate. A new Up platform now stands beyond the signal-box. (J.Watling)

62. This station was renamed Magdalen Road by the Great Eastern Railway on 1st June 1875. In 1966 the porter's duties included preparing tilley lamps to illuminate the platforms, whilst the discerning traveller could still purchase a white LNER 1st class return ticket from the booking office. (J.Watling)

63. Travelling from Wisbech in the 1960s, it was more economic to buy a Cheap Day Return to King's Lynn and alight here beside the Down waiting room, than purchase an Ordinary Return to Magdalen Road. In 1997 this building still served its original purpose, but the goods yard has now been converted into a car park. (J.Watling)

64. There was once a fine example on the Up platform of topiary art, now sadly overgrown. Inclusion of this main-line station in the Wisbech branch closure of September 1968 drew many objections. Following a long campaign, led by railwayman Ron Callaby, the renamed Watlington station reopened as an unstaffed halt on Monday 5th May 1975, and is now served by a frequent electric service to Cambridge and London. (I.C.Allen/ C.Moss)

WIGGENHALL SIDING

Wiggenhall Siding was situated one mile east of Watlington. A wooden ground frame cabin was noted in May 1967, standing on the signal-box site indicated on this map. The passenger station at Magdalen Gate closed on 1st August 1866.

MIDDLE DROVE

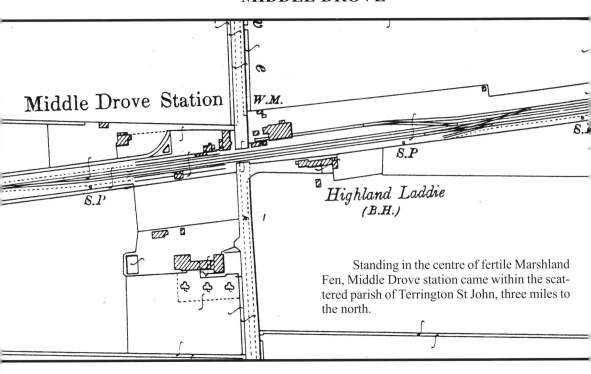

Middle Drove Station   *W.M.*

S.P

S.P

Highland Laddie
(B.H.)

Standing in the centre of fertile Marshland Fen, Middle Drove station came within the scattered parish of Terrington St John, three miles to the north.

65. Conveyance of agricultural produce provided much of the station's revenue. It also had a passing loop, the only one between Watlington and Emneth on this busy goods line. Middle Drove and Emneth goods depots closed on 5th October 1964. (J.Watling)

66. The fireman of BR Standard no. 76031 prepares to collect a single-line tablet for the section to Watlington on Thursday 3rd August 1961. Allocated to 31B March shed in November 1960, this unusual visitor to the branch was transferred to 75A Brighton in November 1962. (J.Watling)

67. The prize winning tidy station was photographed on Tuesday 8th September 1964, but alas no passengers. All stations between Middle Drove and Wisbech became unstaffed halts on 5th June 1967. The Highland Laddie public house can be discerned beyond the Up platform. (J.Watling)

68. Class D16/3 no. 62530 with the 5.56pm from King's Lynn, waits in the loop to cross the 4.14pm Cambridge to King's Lynn train on Thursday 17th July 1958. This locomotive was withdrawn from March shed two months later. (John Langford)

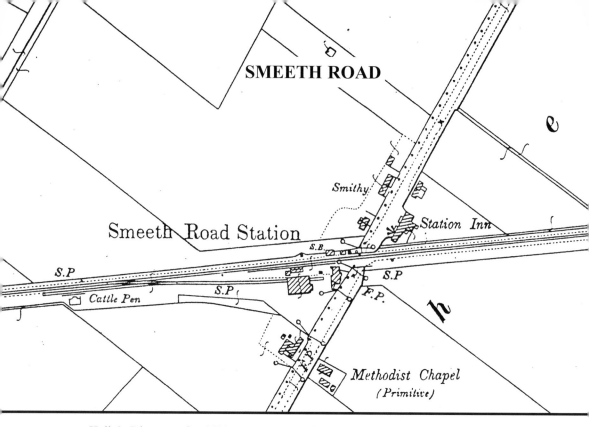

SMEETH ROAD

Smithy

Smeeth Road Station

Station Inn

S.B

S.P

S.P

Cattle Pen

S.P

F.P.

Methodist Chapel
(Primitive)

Kelly's Directory for 1933 names two railway stations within the parish of West Walton, formerly part of Walpole St Peter. Smeeth Road is five miles from the village whilst Ferry station, although just one mile away, is on the far side of the River Nene.

69. Smeeth Road was the only single platform station between Watlington and March. The 1931 census records a village population of 1,048, an increase of just 50 souls since 1851. This view looking east from the level crossing is dated about 1937. (Stations UK)

70. The white-washed platform edge and brick shed outline, introduced to guide passengers during war time blackouts, were still evident on Wednesday 2nd August 1961. Following closure, an agricultural engineering business occupied the goods shed. It has since been converted into flats, with the platform face now serving as a garden wall. (J.Watling)

71. Station Master Eustance Losco Warren began his railway career in 1893 as a clerk at Dersingham. He later worked at Burwell, Barnwell, Stansted and Newmarket stations, before gaining promotion to Smeeth Road in 1918. In 1925 he was also placed in control of Emneth and Middle Drove stations. This portrait followed his appointment as Station Master at Downham Market in August 1930. (Lilian Ream Exhibition Gallery)

72. Smeeth Road box, one of eight between Middle Drove and Coldham, was still standing in 1997, complete with its 15-lever frame. Tales of Tom Hickathrift, the legendary strong man of the Fens, are still retold in this village. Encountering a giant, Tom used his dray wheel as a shield, whilst slaying the giant with the axle-tree. Hickathrift is said to be buried in nearby Tilney All Saints churchyard. (J.Watling)

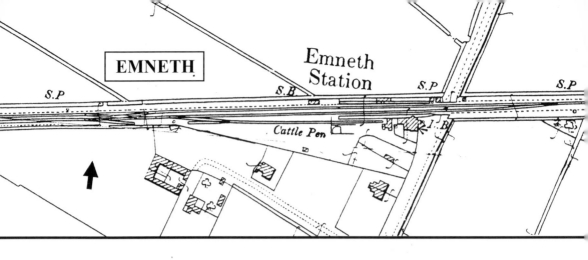

EMNETH

Emneth Station

S.P

S.B

S.P

S.P

Cattle Pen

73. The Watlington to Wisbech branch crossed Marshland Fen in a straight line, resulting in Emneth station standing over one mile north of the village. A class J15 0-6-0 enters the Up platform loop line with a short van train in about 1937. (Stations UK)

74. Emneth signal box alongside the Down platform, stood some distance from the level crossing. This photograph was taken in September 1964 when the late Rev Wilbert Awdry, Emneth's most celebrated resident, was incumbent. Many of his Famous Railway Series books featuring Thomas, Henry, and Gordon were written in the Victorian vicarage alongside St Edmund's parish church. He became one of the world's most successful children's author. (J.Watling)

From August 1883 until December 1927 there were four Great Eastern Railway stations within Emneth parish boundary. This was regarded as the main-line station, for Elm Bridge, Boyce's Bridge and Outwell Basin were depots on the Wisbech & Upwell Tramway. The lower left line is a long siding.

75. We look back towards Watlinfton from the signal-box steps on Tuesday 8th September 1964. A GER carriage body in the goods yard was originally one of 32 vehicles built in 1882/83 for service in the London area. These 27ft four-wheelers were withdrawn between 1915 and 1922, the company finding further use for them as cheap additions to station accommodation. They were also offered for sale to the public at £15 each. (J.Watling)

76. Brush Type 2 no. D5628 heads towards Wisbech, cautiously approaching the tablet apparatus on Wednesday 2nd August 1961. The circular tablet in leather pouch was required to permit Up trains onto the single track to Wisbech, whilst brass key tokens were issued to drivers for the section to Middle Drove. (J.Watling)

WALSOKEN

The Norfolk parish and village of Walsoken were separated from Wisbech by a canal. A one inch to one mile 1st edition map, shows all the original stations on this branch.

77. This station last appeared on a railway timetable in August 1851. The wooden platform was subsequently demolished, but the station house was still standing when photographed in 1949. (National Railway Museum)

5. Upwell towards Wisbech

Route of Wisbech & Upwell Tramway. (Railway Magazine)

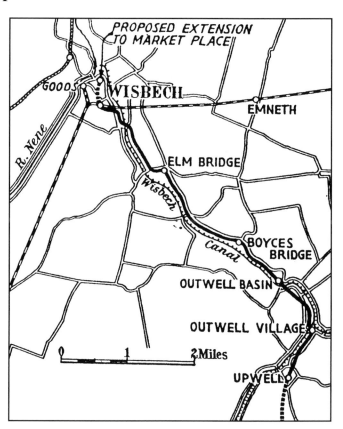

78. Class J70 no. 7136 runs round its train, alongside the former passenger waiting room at Upwell, on Wednesday 15th June 1938. Rev Teddy Boston, former curate of Wisbech St Peter's Church, recalled that "writing sermons never came as a particularly easy job, and quite often I would put the books in a bag, get on the footplate with Charlie Rand, drive the steam tram down to Upwell, and work on the sermon in the little office there. I always found that cleared a mental blockage in a way that nothing else could do". (G.W.Trust/Mark Yardwood coll.)

79. Drewry shunter no. D2201 draws away from Outwell Village Depot with the last tram for Wisbech on Friday 20th May 1966. Although GER bridge no.2337 over Well Creek has now been demolished, and the track lifted, the depot site still remained intact thirty years after closure. In 1994 The Tramyard Trust published plans to establish a small museum on this site. (Lilian Ream Exhibition Gallery)

80. Saturday 9th July 1955 at Outwell Basin Depot saw no. 11101 on the running line, whilst in the back siding long rakes of empty fruit vans await their next consignment of strawberries. Interior walls of the carriage body had originally been decorated with an early English wallpaper. This stylised rose & fleur-de-lis pattern was still visible in the 1980s, behind broken sections of the later wooden panelling. (HMRS/J.J.Davis coll.)

81. Boxes of spring flowers are stacked outside the Foreman's office, as no.11102 arrives at Boyce's Bridge Depot with the afternoon goods to Upwell on Wednesday 27th March 1957. Scotsman Fyfe Robertson, a roving reporter from BBC Television's "Tonight" programme, visited the tramway to compile a short documentary, transmitted in February 1964. This black & white film, and another produced by Anglia Television in 1961, are still in the archives. (W.J.Naunton)

82. The driver, passengers and Conductor/Guard William Collett wait outside the entrance to Inglethorpe Hall, home of local Barclays Bank manager Francis Maltby Bland. He regularly travelled by tram into town, but woe betide if his First Class compartment was not directly opposite the driveway. This photograph is dated between October 1903, when guard's van no. 16 entered tramway service, and the withdrawal of class Y6 no. 131 in September 1907. (A.Tustin coll.)

83. The 12.55pm inaugural diesel-hauled tram to Upwell crosses over Wisbech Canal at New Common Bridge on Wednesday 4th June 1952. No. 11102 is also about to cross the southern town and county boundary into the parish of Emneth, Norfolk. A comprehensive survey of the Wisbech Tram and Canal can be found in the companion album *Branch Line to Upwell*. (M.N.Bland)

K 8232

G. E. R.
WISBECH & OUTWELL TRAMWAY

WISBECH to UPWELL

Fare **4**D First Class **4**D UPWELL to WISBECH

This Ticket is issued subject to the Regulations
of the Company. It is
available for a SINGLE
journey only—on the Car
where issued. It must be
produced on demand of
the Conductor or other
Officials of the Company
and given up on leaving
the Car. Any passenger
attempting to use this
Ticket for a second
journey will be liable to
Prosecution.

		morn	morn	morn	even.	even.	even.	even.	**NS** even.	**SO** even.
WISBECH ....dep.		7 30	9 30	10 55	12 40	2 30	4 25	6 20	8 30	9 0
Elm Depot— — — „		7 41	9 41	11 6	12 51	2 41	4 36	6 31	8 41	9 11
Boyce's Depot .... „		7 51	9 51	11 16	1 1	2 51	4 50	6 41	8 51	9 21
Outwell Basin— — „		7 57	9 57	11 22	1 7	2 57	4 56	6 47	8 57	9 27
Outwell Village ...... „		8 3	10 3	11 28	1 13	3 3	5 2	6 53	9 3	9 33
UPWELL — —arr.		8 9	10 9	11 34	1 19	3 9	5 8	6 59	9 9	9 39

NS Not Saturdays.   **SO** Saturdays only.

January 1923

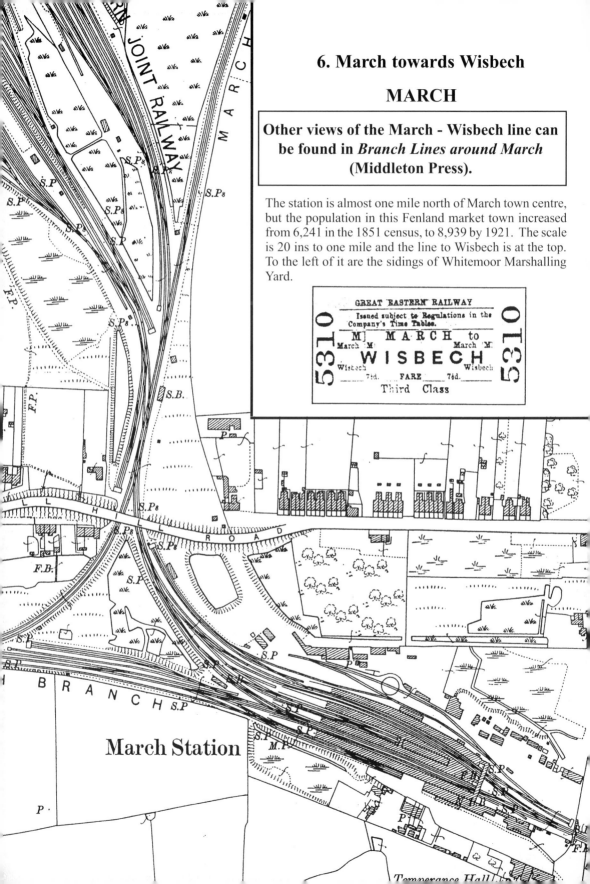

JOINT RAILWAY

6. March towards Wisbech

MARCH

Other views of the March - Wisbech line can be found in *Branch Lines around March* (Middleton Press).

The station is almost one mile north of March town centre, but the population in this Fenland market town increased from 6,241 in the 1851 census, to 8,939 by 1921. The scale is 20 ins to one mile and the line to Wisbech is at the top. To the left of it are the sidings of Whitemoor Marshalling Yard.

GREAT EASTERN RAILWAY

Issued subject to Regulations in the Company's Time Tables.

5310

MJ   M A R C H   to
March 'M'   March 'M'
Wisbech   W I S B E C H   Wisbech
7½d.   FARE   7½d.
Third Class

5310

HILL ROAD

F.B.

BRANCH

March Station

M.P.

Temperance Hall

84. March station forecourt on Sunday 12th April 1981. The original Eastern Counties Railway station stood to the east of this building, adjacent to Station Road level crossing. In November 1885 the GER built this larger structure, the adjacent ECR building being retained as a Station Master's residence. (A.C.Ingram)

85. We now look west from platform 6 in about 1955. A van rests against the bufferstops in bay platform 4, frequented by local trains to Wisbech and King's Lynn. By 1997 the ornate valancing and almost half the canopy had been removed, but the station buildings remain, complete with several examples of etched glass windows. (Stations UK)

86. Class D16/3 no. 62618, formerly LNER no. 8787, had always been kept immaculate by Cambridge shed to haul Royal trains from London King's Cross to Wolferton. Now this former Royal Claud has been relegated to shunting vans at March on Wednesday 30th May 1951. (M.N.Bland)

87. The Wisbech and March Railway Action Committee (WAMRAC) chartered an excursion from Wisbech to Cambridge on Saturday 23rd September 1978. Founded in May 1974 and led by Lt Col John Bolam, the organisation campaigned for the reintroduction of passenger services on the goods branch to Wisbech. (A.C.Ingram)

88. A view north from the station in 1970 includes Norwood Road bridge, formerly Mill Hill Road. Road overbridges are rare in the flat fens as they require steep approaches. This water tower is a remnant of the former locomotive shed, demolished in 1885 and replaced by a larger structure alongside Whitemoor yard. By 1985 track rationalisation required Down trains to shunt at Whitemoor Junction to gain access to the Wisbech line, with a maximum speed on the branch of 25mph. (A.C.Ingram)

89. Norwood Bridge offered an ideal vantage point for trainspotters, although Thursday 12th March 1953 appears to have been rather quiet. The GN&GE line to Spalding curves west to pass between the Up and Down marshalling yards, now occupied by Whitemoor Prison. The double track to Wisbech can be seen heading north past the massive 147-lever Whitemoor Junction signal-box. (M.N.Bland)

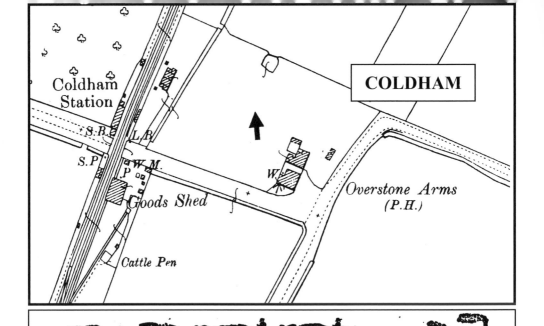

COLDHAM

Coldham
Station

S.B. L.B.

S.P.

W.M.

P.

Goods Shed

Cattle Pen

Overstone Arms
(P.H.)

EASTERN COUNTIES RAILWAY

OPENING OF THE
WISBECH BRANCH

An Excursion Train

WILL LEAVE

WISBECH FOR ELY AND CAMBRIDGE,

On Monday the 3d of May,

Calling at MARCH as follows :—

From WISBECH	at ..	9	o'Clock A.M.
,, MARCH	at ..	9.30	,,
,, ELY	at ..	10.15	,,
Arriving at CAMBRIDGE	at ..	11.0	,,

AND WILL RETURN

From CAMBRIDGE	at ..	6	o'Clock P.M.
,, ELY	at ..	6.45	,,
,, MARCH	at ..	7.30	,,
Arriving at WISBECH	at ..	8.0	,,

FARES

TO ELY OR CAMBRIDGE AND BACK.

First Class, 6s.—Second Class, 4s.—Third Class, 2s. 6d.

☞ TICKETS may be obtained at the RAILWAY STATION, on and after the
30th of APRIL.

N.B. A Limited Number only will be issued.

By order,

C. P. RONEY, SECRETARY.

April 26th, 1847.

(upper left)

The village of Coldham, four miles north of March, became an ecclesiastical parish on 10th July 1874. A population of 350 in 1871 had increased to 425 by 1921. There was a one-ton crane in the goods shed.

90. The signal box, opened in 1886, and station house standing alongside the Down line were recorded on 16th October 1962. Coldham possessed the only timber station buildings on this branch. The design, similar to Stonea, Manea and Black Bank stations on the March to Ely line, may have been influenced by unstable soil conditions. (J.Watling)

91. A hay cart is being led along Station Road towards Cherrytree Hill Farm. The Co-operative Wholesale Society Limited were the principal landowners, the chief crops being wheat, barley, oats, potatoes, along with brown and white mustard. Horse stable manure, or "London Muck", was imported by train into the Wisbech area, and spread on the land. Instead of being straw-based it was a mixture of wood shavings and sawdust. (Lilian Ream Exhibition Gallery)

92. Class J15 no. 65356 with an Up afternoon train passes the goods yard. The driver, Charlie Rand, regularly worked Wisbech main-line, tramway, and harbour branch trains. In his Railway Series stories, Rev Awdry based the character of Charlie Sand, Edward the Blue Engine's driver, on Charlie Rand. (P.J.Lynch)

93. Looking south, a slight curve is noticeable on an otherwise 8 mile straight run between March and Wisbech. A former signalman recalled the custom of keeping a large Bible in each signal-box for staff to read, with another copy for passengers in the Waiting Room. Goods facilities were withdrawn on 19th April 1965, and from Monday 7th March 1966 passenger trains no longer called at Coldham. (J.Watling)

WALDERSEA SIDING

The Great Eastern Railway opened their siding at Waldersea on Tuesday 20th November 1900. There are still seven level crossings between Whitemoor and Wisbech East Goods. Two half-barrier, one ungated, and four crew-operated gates (including Waldersea) in addition to a number of occupation crossings.

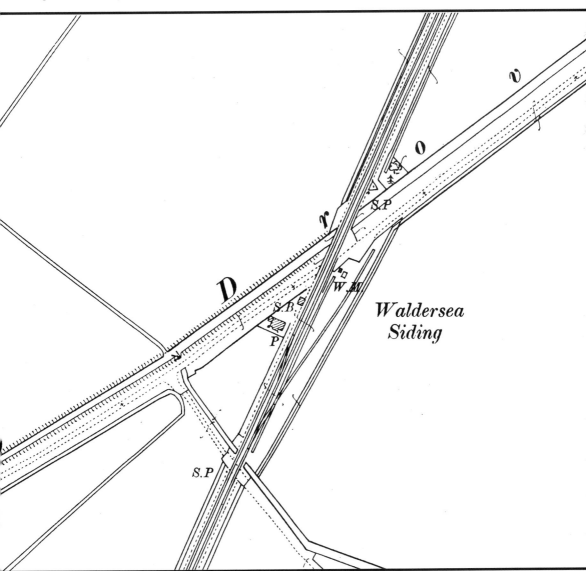

Waldersea Siding

94. Arthur Randall began his railway career at Magdalen Road station in 1918, after spending his youth catching moles with his father. In 1925 he was appointed porter-signalman at Waldersea with responsibility for the crossing gates, siding, and 20-lever signal-box. Following his retirement in April 1965 Arthur returned to mole-catching, covering 4,000 acres of the Fens.
(Lilian Ream Exhibition Gallery)

95. Class B1 no. 61095 passes Waldersea with an Up goods train on Monday 20th March 1961. In December 1965 the author stood in this box and witnessed possibly the last steam working on the Wisbech branch, as a B1 worked light engine to King's Lynn for carriage heating duties. (J.Watling)

NEW BRIDGE LANE CROSSING

96. Gatekeeper Olive Harris appeared on the BBC Television panel game "What's My Line" in 1957, where she acted a mime of her daily work. The celebrity panel of Lady Isobel Barnett, Barbara Kelly, Gilbert Harding and David Nixon, failed to guess her profession, and she was therefore awarded a certificate by presenter Eamonn Andrews. (Lilian Ream Exhibition Gallery)

Extract from Waldersea Siding signing-on register. Note the entry for Italian Prisoners of War from the nearby Friday Bridge camp and that they had no time to digest their lunch.

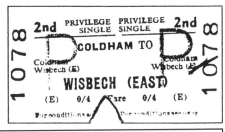

Wednesday July 4th 1945

Name	Grade	Time on Duty From	To	Meal Interval	Total Time Worked
A R Randell	Ptr Sig	8.0	8.0	1hr	11.00
G A Peachey	Gds Porter	8.0	5.30	1 hr	8.30
3 P.O.W.		10.0	4.0	30 mins	

WEASENHAM LANE CROSSING

97. Class J15 0-6-0 no. 7888 stands beside the wreckage of an American Essex car, hit by a train at the crossing on Tuesday 10th July 1934. Two Wisbech men in the car jumped clear just in time as their vehicle was pushed nearly 50 yards along the track towards March. The crossing keeper's cottage stands in the background. (Lilian Ream Exhibition Gallery)

98. A panorama from the crossing towards Wisbech Goods Junction on Saturday 5th August 1972, shows that the Down main-line rails had recently been lifted. In February 1954 four additional levers were added to the 27-lever Wisbech Goods Junction signal-box. These controlled the Metal Box siding and Charlie Coulson's Weasenham Lane crossing gates. (A.C.Ingram)

99. Opened in 1953, the Metal Box factory produced 30 million cans a week for all East Anglian vegetable and meat producers. Assembled open-top cans were packed into boxes, then loaded into goods vans on the left. Wagons of tin waste "slitter trims" in the centre road were sent to South Wales for recycling. Coils of tinplate still arrive at the factory by rail, but waste is now dispatched by road. (Lilian Ream Exhibition Gallery)

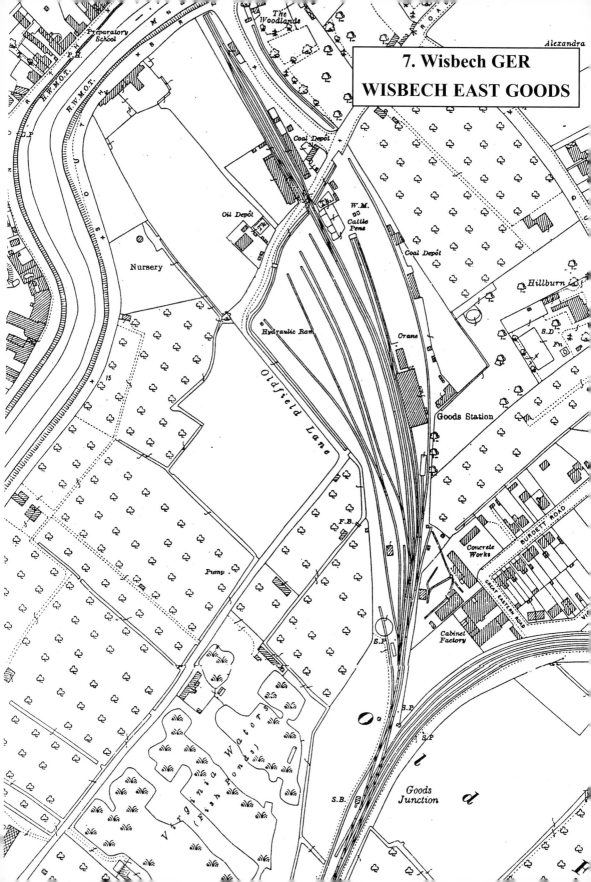

7. Wisbech GER
WISBECH EAST GOODS

Alexandra

The Woodlands

Preparatory School

H.W.M.O.T.

P.H.

H.W.M.O.T.

Coal Depot

Oil Depôt

W.M. Cattle Pens

Coal Depôt

Nursery

Hillburn

S.D.

Hydraulic Ram

Crane

Goods Station

Oldfield Lane

Concrete Works

BURDETT ROAD

F.B.

Pump

GREAT EASTERN ROAD

Cabinet Factory

S.P.

Waters (Fish Ponds)

S.P.

S.P.

Virginia

S.B.

Goods Junction

d

100. Over sixty years before the Channel Tunnel opened, Wisbech was exporting fruit by train direct to the continent. In November 1930 up to ten wagons a day, each loaded with five tons of loose apples, travelled via the Harwich-Hook of Holland train ferry to destinations in France, Belgium and Germany. Local growers found this route actually cheaper than sending their produce to markets in London. (Lilian Ream Exhibition Gallery)

A 1927 survey of Wisbech East Goods, includes cattle pens on the original 1847 passenger station site. An impressive piece of silverware, commemorating the line's opening, featured on the BBC Television series "Antiques Roadshow" in 1993. The crane was of six-ton capacity.

101. Class J15 no. 65356, allocated to 31B March, shunting on the Down road, with the Cooperative Wholesale Society Preserve Works on the far side of Somers Road. Under-Shunter Sid Bellamy (with pole) and Checker Fred Petts are in the yard, with Head Shunter Cyril Taylor and Driver Albert South on the footplate. (P.J.Lynch)

102. In 1975 around 8,000 tons of freight were dispatched by rail from Wisbech, with Metal Box, Spillers, and coal merchants receiving 45,000 tons at the Wisbech terminus. A wide range of diesel motive power, including classes 08, 20, 31 and 47, have worked this traffic over the past 25 years. In 1997 a class 56 with Leicester-based driver and two trainmen regularly hauled the Spillers Pet Food train. (A.C.Ingram)

103. Seed potato merchants Clifford Cross appear to be overwhelmed with business in this posed photograph of Upper Hill Street. Their whitewashed offices on the left formerly housed the Wisbech Grammar School, where anti-slavery campaigner Thomas Clarkson was born in 1760. Great Eastern drays are on the right, with rival Midland Railway covered wagons in the background. (Wisbech & Fenland Museum)

104. Boarding the *SS Lady Alice Lambton*, passengers discovered she was not an elegant paddle steamer as depicted in the poster, but a 700 ton collier. The vessel owner Richard Young treated his 1000 guests "in the most handsome manner", with dancing 'tween decks and a brass band from Cambridge. He was a director of several railway companies, including the Great Eastern, and his home, Osborn House, stands in the background. (Samuel Smith/Wisbech & Fenland Museum)

105. Local timber merchants English Bros established their business alongside the River Nene in 1843. A scene of desolation greeted their employees on Thursday 25th October 1928 following a major fire. This two-acre site had contained five drying sheds and stacks of wood before flames took hold early Wednesday evening. A railway footbridge linked the nine cottages in Osborn Road, threatened by the flames, with Mount Pleasant Road. (Lilian Ream Exhibition Gallery)

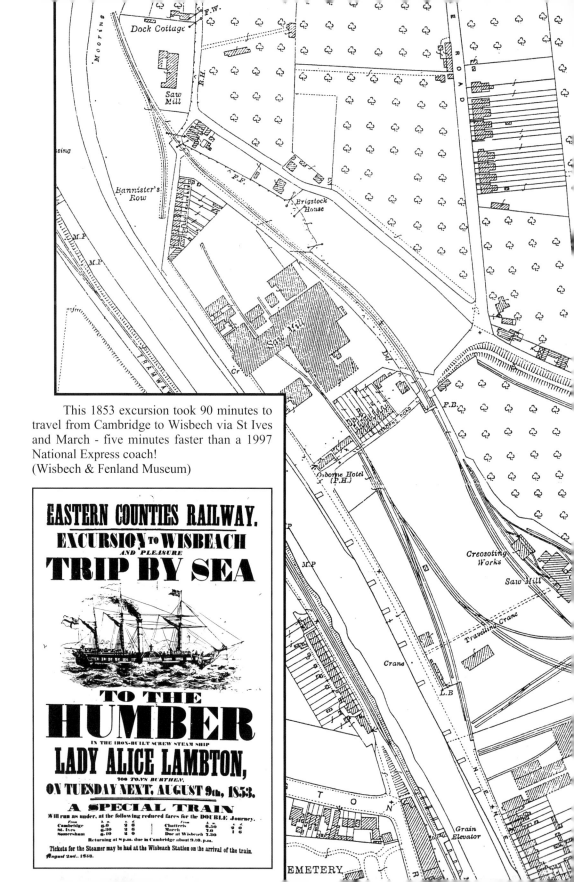

This 1853 excursion took 90 minutes to travel from Cambridge to Wisbech via St Ives and March - five minutes faster than a 1997 National Express coach!
(Wisbech & Fenland Museum)

EASTERN COUNTIES RAILWAY.
EXCURSION TO WISBEACH
AND PLEASURE
TRIP BY SEA
TO THE
HUMBER
IN THE IRON-BUILT SCREW STEAM SHIP
LADY ALICE LAMBTON,
700 TONS BURTHEN;
ON TUESDAY NEXT, AUGUST 9th, 1853.
A SPECIAL TRAIN
Will run as under, at the following reduced fares for the DOUBLE Journey.

From	s. d.	s. d.	From	s. d.	s. d.
Cambridge	6.0	4.30	Chatteris	4.30	2.6
St. Ives	5.30	2.6	March	7.0	1.6
Somersham	5.40	2.0	Due at Wisbech	7.30	

Returning at 8 p.m. due in Cambridge about 9.30. p.m.
Tickets for the Steamer may be had at the Wisbeach Station on the arrival of the train.
August 2nd. 1853.

106. This 1929 publicity photograph illustrates some of the products, including windmills, that English Bros manufactured. In the 1920s they began importing Aspen logs from the Baltic into Wisbech Port to produce "chip" baskets for local fruit growers. During wartime the company also assembled ammunition boxes. (Lilian Ream Exhibition Gallery)

The Eastern Counties Railway obtained powers to construct this branch from Wisbech station to the Harbour in 1852, but it was a Great Eastern Railway train that first travelled on the line in 1862. The sidings in Eastfield serviced the Wisbech Gas Light and Coke Co. This 1927 survey shows the extensive system at its peak.

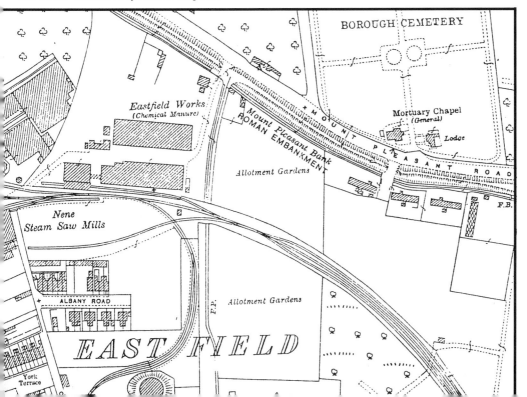

107. Wisbech became the largest timber-importer on the East Coast by the late 19th century, with 76,968 tons of hewn and sawn logs arriving in 1897. A GWR 5-plank wagon is loaded with timber within J.T.Stanton's drying shed in 1932. (Lilian Ream Exhibition Gallery)

108. Class J15 no. 65474 shunts a train of English Bros timber in 1958, watched by Shunter Bob Green and Foreman Bob Brown. A narrow gauge wagonway and traverser, within the English Bros complex, carried loaded timber wagons to pressurised creosote and "celcure" treatment plants. In winter a tang of Seville oranges from the adjacent Chivers marmalade factory drifted over the harbour branch. (Lilian Ream Exhibition Gallery)

109. Wisbech Produce Canners Ltd opened a pea canning factory on Thursday 27th June 1929. Sidings were constructed by the LNER to accept the daily output of 100,000 cans. Managing Director S W Smedley imported coal for the factory boilers in his Private Owner wagons. (Lilian Ream Exhibition Gallery)

110. Len Wilson, in the foreground, directs his Permanent Way gang following a minor derailment on Monday 28th June 1954. The mishap, which occurred at 11.30am alongside the pedestrian crossing linking DeHavilland Road and Mount Pleasant, was resolved by lunchtime. Porter Ray Laud cycled ahead of each harbour train to open crossing gates on Lynn Road, Park Road, Norwich Road and Ramnoth Road. (Lilian Ream Exhibition Gallery)

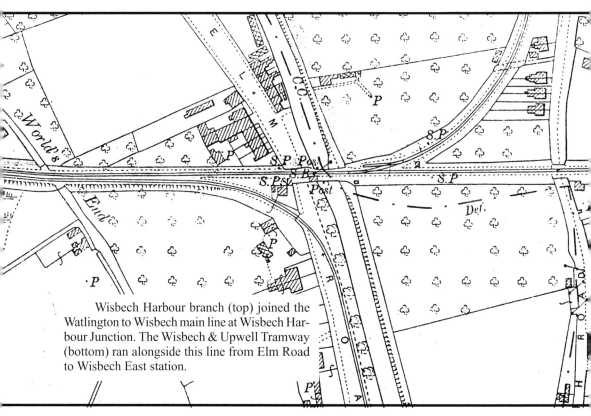

Wisbech Harbour branch (top) joined the Watlington to Wisbech main line at Wisbech Harbour Junction. The Wisbech & Upwell Tramway (bottom) ran alongside this line from Elm Road to Wisbech East station.

111. Drewry shunter no. D2202 approaches Wisbech Harbour Junction, now the site of Wisbech Fire Station, with four wagons from the branch. The main line to King's Lynn is on the right, with Ramnoth Road level crossing and keeper's cottage in the background. (I.C.Allen/C.Moss)

112. The Wisbech & Upwell Tramway is in the foreground while in the background is Wisbech Harbour Junction box. Signalman Arthur Barrett is beside the main line gates in Great Eastern days. This box was later demoted to a crossing box, with Harbour line points and signals released by the sections tablet, brought from Wisbech East by a station inspector. The tablet was inserted into the auxiliary tablet Instrument for the points to be released, and then returned to Wisbech East. The whole process was repeated when the train left the branch. (L.Baxter coll.)

113. With its side valancing almost scraping the tarmac, D2201 cautiously crosses Elm Road with the afternoon tram from Upwell in May 1966. A redundant Permanent Way trolley aboard the leading wagon confirms that the tramway's end is nigh. (Lilian Ream Exhibition Gallery)

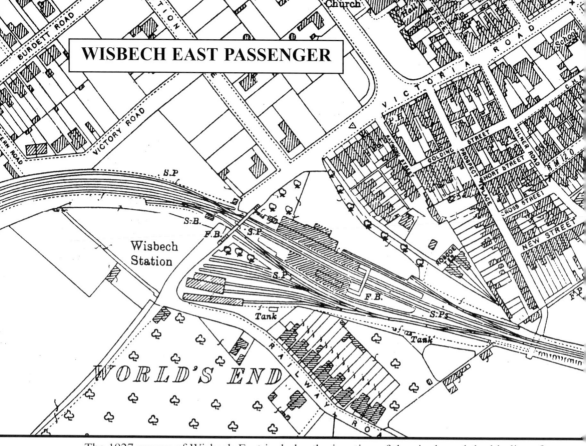

WISBECH EAST PASSENGER

Wisbech
Station

WORLD'S END

The 1927 survey of Wisbech East includes the junction of the single and double lines from Watlington and March respectively. Surveys of this station for 1888 and 1902 can be found in the companion album Branch Line to Upwell.

August 1866

GREAT EASTERN RAILWAY.
CAMBRIDGE LINE.

CHEAP EXCURSION TICKETS TO LONDON are issued from certain of the Company's Stations every TUESDAY, available for the RETURN JOURNEY on the SATURDAY or SATURDAY WEEK following the day of issue.

Monthly and Weekly Tickets are also issued from certain of the principal stations to HARWICH, ALDBOROUGH, YARMOUTH, LOWESTOFT, and HUNSTANTON.

For particulars see hand-bills, and published time books of the company.
(By Order   R. MOSELEY, General Manager.

GREAT EASTERN RAILWAY.
EXCURSIONS TO THE SEA-SIDE.
EXCURSION TICKETS
Are Issued EVERY MONDAY and THURSDAY, to
HUNSTANTON AND BACK,
AS UNDER:

From WISBECH, EMNETH, SMEETH ROAD, MIDDLE DROVE, MAGDALEN GATE, AND WATLINGTON, On MONDAYS and THURSDAYS by Train leaving Wisbech at 7·40 a.m., returning from Hunstanton at 4.15 and 7·45 p.m.

FARES TO HUNSTANTON AND BACK.

FIRST CLASS.	SECOND CLASS.	THIRD CLASS.
4s. 0d.	3s. 0d.	2s. 0d.

N.B.—Refreshment Rooms at Hunstanton.

BY ORDER,   R. MOSELEY, General Manager.

114. In his autobiography Rev Teddy Boston remembered the fascination of Wisbech Station signal-box "because you could never tell what was going to happen next". Class J70 no. 7136 approaches Wisbech East on the tram road with a goods tram for Upwell in the 1930s. The author recalls many happy hours working the box under supervision from signalman Bob Fitzjohn.
(G.W.Trust/Mark Yardwood coll.)

An enamel double-sided nameplate, designed by the LNER to hang beneath platform gas mantles. British Railways totem nameplates were not issued to intermediate stations on this branch.
(Wisbech & Fenland Museum)

115. Five class J70 0-6-0 steam tram engines, together with four class Y6 0-4-0s, were stationed at Wisbech in August 1936. J70 no. 7130 was photographed by C. Hamilton Ellis in the 1930s, alongside the coal stage at Wisbech Tram Shed. Driver Charlie Rand recalled "She's the dud one, 130, she never would steam properly. Used to have to stop and have a blow up with her many a time". (National Railway Museum)

116. Crowds of people turned out on Sunday 30th July 1939 to give a hearty send-off to "C" Company of the 1st and 2nd Battalions, The Cambridgeshire Regiment. The Territorials are leaving Wisbech for camp at Shorncliffe in Kent, just five weeks before the declaration of war. Captured at Singapore in February 1942, they worked on the infamous Burma Railway until the Japanese surrender in August 1945. (Lilian Ream Exhibition Gallery)

117. Station interior looking towards March in 1953, with a porter transferring pigeon baskets to the Up platform. That distinctive news-stand aroma wafts along the Down platform, where each strawberry season the Waiting Room became an office for additional goods clerks. A 20mph speed restriction prevailed on the tight left-hand curve to Wisbech Goods Junction. (National Railway Museum)

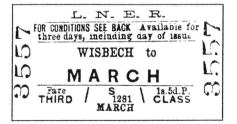

118. Arriving at the Down platform with a local Sunday train in April 1953, Cambridge-based Claud no. 62567 has run around its train and now stands beside the Bookroom. Ten minutes before departure, the train will reverse onto the Up line for the return to March. Derby Lightweight and Craven diesel multiple-units operated local services in The Fens from 3rd November 1958, effectively sealing the fate of remaining B12 and Claud Hamilton steam locomotives.
(National Railway Museum)

119. TV cameraman Lloyd Hobson prepares to film D2201, with Driver Albert South at the controls, hauling the final tram through Wisbech East station on Friday 20th May 1966. He returned in November 1995 to film the Tram and Canal Exhibition at Wisbech & Fenland Museum.
(Lilian Ream Exhibition Gallery)

120. Wisbech Station signal-box board and lever plates, on display at the Wisbech & Fenland Museum in 1983. TV and radio personality Johnny Morris shares a joke with the author during a visit to the Tramway Centenary exhibition. In the 1950s he narrated stories of Toby the Tram Engine, written by Rev Wilbert Awdry, and based on that most famous of all Branch Lines around Wisbech.
(Eastern Daily Press)

MP Middleton Press

Easebourne Lane, Midhurst, West Sussex. GU29 9AZ Tel: 01730 813169 Fax: 01730 812601
... *WRITE OR PHONE FOR OUR LATEST LIST* ...

BRANCH LINES

Branch Line to Allhallows
Branch Lines to Alton
Branch Lines around Ascot
Branch Line to Ashburton
Branch Lines around Bodmin
Branch Line to Bude
Branch Lines around Canterbury
Branch Line to Cheddar
Branch Lines to East Grinstead
Branch Lines to Effingham Junction
Branch Line to Fairford
Branch Line to Hawkhurst
Branch Line to Hayling
Branch Lines to Horsham
Branch Line to Ilfracombe
Branch Lines to Longmoor
Branch Line to Lyme Regis
Branch Line to Lynton
Branch Lines around Midhurst
Branch Line to Minehead
Branch Lines to Newport (IOW)
Branch Line to Padstow
Branch Lines around Plymouth
Branch Lines around Portmadoc 1923-46
Branch Lines around Porthmadog 1954-94
Branch Lines to Seaton & Sidmouth
Branch Line to Selsey
Branch Lines around Sheerness
Branch Line to Southwold
Branch Line to Swanage
Branch Line to Tenterden
Branch Lines to Torrington
Branch Line to Upwell
Branch Lines around Wimborne
Branch Lines around Wisbech

SOUTH COAST RAILWAYS

Ashford to Dover
Brighton to Eastbourne
Chichester to Portsmouth
Dover to Ramsgate
Portsmouth to Southampton
Ryde to Ventnor
Worthing to Chichester

SOUTHERN MAIN LINES

Bromley South to Rochester
Charing Cross to Orpington
Crawley to Littlehampton
Dartford to Sittingbourne
East Croydon to Three Bridges
Epsom to Horsham
Exeter to Barnstaple
Exeter to Tavistock
Faversham to Dover
Haywards Heath to Seaford
London Bridge to East Croydon
Orpington to Tonbridge
Sittingbourne to Ramsgate
Swanley to Ashford
Tavistock to Plymouth
Victoria to Bromley South
Waterloo to Windsor

Woking to Portsmouth
Woking to Southampton
Yeovil to Exeter

COUNTRY RAILWAY ROUTES

Bath to Evercreech Junction
Bournemouth to Evercreech Jn.
Burnham to Evercreech Junction
Croydon to East Grinstead
East Kent Light Railway
Fareham to Salisbury
Frome to Bristol
Guildford to Redhill
Porthmadog to Blaenau
Reading to Basingstoke
Reading to Guildford
Redhill to Ashford
Salisbury to Westbury
Strood to Paddock Wood
Taunton to Barnstaple
Westbury to Bath
Woking to Alton
Yeovil to Dorchester

GREAT RAILWAY ERAS

Ashford from Steam to Eurostar
Festiniog in the Fifties
Festiniog in the Sixties

LONDON SUBURBAN RAILWAYS

Caterham and Tattenham Corner
Clapham Jn. to Beckenham Jn.
Crystal Palace and Catford Loop
East London Line
Finsbury Park to Alexandra Palace
Holborn Viaduct to Lewisham
Lines around Wimbledon
London Bridge to Addiscombe
Mitcham Junction Lines
North London Line
South London Line
West Croydon to Epsom
West London Line
Willesden Junction to Richmond
Wimbledon to Epsom

STEAM PHOTOGRAPHERS

O.J.Morris's Southern Railways 1919-59

STEAMING THROUGH

Steaming through Cornwall
Steaming through East Sussex
Steaming through the Isle of Wight
Steaming through Kent
Steaming through West Hants
Steaming through West Sussex

TRAMWAY CLASSICS

Aldgate & Stepney Tramways
Barnet & Finchley Tramways
Bath Tramways
Bournemouth & Poole Tramways

Brighton's Tramways
Bristol's Tramways
Camberwell & W.Norwood Tramways
Croydon's Tramways
Clapham & Streatham Tramways
Dover's Tramways
East Ham & West Ham Tramways
Eltham & Woolwich Tramways
Embankment & Waterloo Tramways
Enfield & Wood Green Tramways
Exeter & Taunton Tramways
Gosport & Horndean Tramways
Greenwich & Dartford Tramways
Hampstead & Highgate Tramways
Hastings Tramways
Holborn & Finsbury Tramways
Ilford & Barking Tramways
Kingston & Wimbledon Tramways
Lewisham & Catford Tramways
Liverpool Tramways 1. Eastern Routes
Maidstone & Chatham Tramways
North Kent Tramways
Portsmouth's Tramways
Reading Tramways
Seaton & Eastbourne Tramways
Southampton Tramways
Southend-on-sea Tramways
Southwark & Deptford Tramways
Stamford Hill Tramways
Thanet's Tramways
Victoria & Lambeth Tramways
Walthamstow & Leyton Tramways
Wandsworth & Battersea Tramways

TROLLEYBUS CLASSICS

Croydon's Trolleybuses
Hastings Trolleybuses
Maidstone Trolleybuses
Woolwich & Dartford Trolleybuses

WATERWAY ALBUMS

Hampshire Waterways
Kent and East Sussex Waterways
London's Lost Route to the Sea
London to Portsmouth Waterway
Surrey Waterways

MILITARY BOOKS

Battle over Portsmouth
Battle over Sussex 1940
Blitz over Sussex 1941-42
Bombers over Sussex 1943-45
Bognor at War
Military Defence of West Sussex
Secret Sussex Resistance

OTHER BOOKS

Brickmaking in Sussex
Garraway Father & Son
Index to all Stations
Industrial Railways of the South East
London Chatham & Dover Railway

SOUTHERN RAILWAY VIDEO

War on the Line